46 of 50

Signed by
Author and Designer

Guinea Bastard: Personal Essays

Joe Pagetta

To my mother.
What else would you expect from a nice Italian boy?

"It ain't no sin to be glad you're alive"
    Bruce Springsteen, "Badlands"

"You have to learn everything you can ... and then you have to forget
it, and what you can't forget will create the foundation of your work."
    Paul Auster, *4321*

CONTENTS

IN THE DARK

Cockroaches scatter when you turn the lights on. Water bugs, their older, larger and blacker cousins, do not. They just stand there looking at you. I'm not sure if they're stupid and playing dead — doubtful, since their younger cousins are very bright — or tough and just don't care. I grew up with water bugs.

My second floor bedroom in Jersey City, New Jersey had a radiator with pipes that extended down through the floors to the basement, where a drain sat in case the water heater overflowed or the basement flooded. I never actually saw it happen, but I hypothesized that the water bugs came up through the drain, crawled up the radiator pipe into my room and hung out on my desk or wall, or shelves, or when they were feeling particularly friendly, my bed. I fell asleep in fear many nights, only to wake intuitively, jump out of bed and flick on the lights to confront my guests. I hated them. They soiled endless soles on my shoes, used up paper towels, and genuinely made my life miserable. I tried to understand them, but I'm not sure I ever did, because I never knew what they wanted. Aliens visit other worlds for a reason, yes?

Now that I'm an adult, I suffer night terrors sometimes. I wake up in a fit and think there are spiders descending on me from the ceiling or hovering in front of me. I throw the sheets off in a panic, jump out of bed and put the lights on, only to find nothing.

The thing is, I have no beef with spiders. No phobia. No history. Why spiders, and not the nemeses of my youth? I guess I'll never know. Sometimes the motivations of the mind, like the motivations of water bugs to climb two floors to taunt a young child, are meant to be a mystery.

It's the same with memoir. I don't know why certain events in my life remain more vivid than others. Why some haunt me, while others comfort. Or even why some seem like they'd make good stories and ought to be written down and shared.

What's most fascinating is that imaginary spiders descending from a ceiling remind me of water bugs climbing up radiator pipes. Which puts me back in the bedroom I grew up in, off the kitchen on the second floor of a two-family house in Jersey City Heights, with a window overlooking the back of the house where we kept the garbage cans. I hear my sister on the phone, whispering with her boyfriend in the middle of the night, the cord stretching from the kitchen. I can hear my father storming toward us from us his bedroom on the opposite side of the apartment. I see him ripping the phone off the wall and throwing it in the garbage. But not until after my sister tells her boyfriend, "I gotta go. My father's coming."

In the morning I see the horrible orange and black patterned carpet in the kitchen. I see a book about cats in the produce drawer of the refrigerator, put there by me while sleepwalking, supposedly because I like cats and miss the stray one I took care of for a while. Out the window of my bedroom I see my grandfather swatting at flies by the garbage cans with a rolled-up newspaper. Thwack! Clang! He's wearing an orange polo shirt. Or perhaps I think it's orange because that's the color of the vinyl chair he likes to sit in down in the finished basement.

This is how it goes in writing our life stories. One things leads to another and we're surprised to learn that we remember as much as we do. So we keep going, plumbing the depths, and perhaps the debts, too, in search of some meaning and understanding as to how we got here. How we got out of that jam. How we got through that time. But often, what we discover is not always what we remember. Madeleine L'Engle primarily wrote fiction, but I think this quote about her process applies equally to writing memoir.

> *Writing fiction is definitely a universe disturber, and for the writer, first of all. My books push me and prod me and make me ask questions I might otherwise avoid. I start a book, having lived with the characters for several years, during the writing of other books, and I have a pretty good idea of where the story is going and what I hope it's going to say. And then, once I get deep into the writing, unexpected things begin to happen, things which make me question, and which sometimes really shake my universe.* °

In place of fiction, put "memoir" or "personal essay." In place of "the characters," put "myself" or "the people in my life" and you'll know what I mean.

1 REALITY SHOWS

Camel Jockey. Big Nose. Freckle Face. Doughboy. Nigger George. Purgatory. Downtown. These were the names of the kids in my neighborhood. I, of course, when I wasn't being called Greaseball or Guinea Bastard, was called Spaghetti, or Spaghetti-head, or some variation on the spaghetti thing, which, considering my last name, was quite inspired. The same could be said for the creative energy that went into Big Nose's and Freckle Face's monikers. None of us made up our names. I would have preferred DiMaggio, or Broadway Joe, or the Italian Stallion, but things didn't work that way. Your name was bestowed upon you at some point – based on your real name, your ethnicity, your physical appearance or something dumb you once said or did – and it stuck.

Whether or not you liked your name didn't matter. The most important thing was that you had a name. It meant you existed on the block, were part of its concrete and tar. You belonged. If Camel Jockey threw deep in a game of touch football in the street and called out to "Catch, it Spaghetti!!!" you knew you better. When you did, it was thrilling. The names were strange urban terms of endearment. How else do you explain being able to call someone who could have easily kicked all our asses Nigger George? Thinking about it now, I'm mortified at the insensitivity of it all. But that's the way it was. Camel Jockey was no slouch either.

Back then, reality was fluid, like a drone flying about the neighborhood and stopping every dozen feet to capture a photo and declare, "This is what the whole thing looks like." Reality was one thing when you were on the corner, choosing sides for stickball or wondering if the blacktop was hot enough to carve in a bottle caps board. It was a completely different thing in your house—one usually the inverse of the other. Freckle Face was one of the leaders on the block. Someone you didn't want to fuck with if you could help it. But within the confines of his apartment, it was clear he was scared shit of his parents and hated being home. His entire body language would change when he walked through the front door of his building, as if the vestibule was really a telephone booth with one way in and another way out. Superman always used the door that faced the street; Clark Kent the hallway.

In between these two states, you lived in your head. In my apartment and around my family I was the youngest, the goofiest, the nerdiest and the "good one" trying his best to avoid a house overrun by gamblers, abusers, yellers and thieves. On the street I was the smart one, the fast one, the nice one who got along with everyone and, on one occasion, the one who hit the farthest stickball shot in the history of the neighborhood (three sewer plates!). In my head I was Don Mattingly's younger brother, or Jets wide receiver Wesley Walker if he were white, Italian and lived in the Jersey City Heights. I was Huck and Jim's rafting partner, WNEW DJ Scott Muni's sole confidant and Go-Go Belinda Carlisle's soulmate. If I had time, I might have even been St. Francis reincarnated and saved all the animals in the world.

Sometimes, I would close the door to my bedroom and spread my head out a little. I'd listen to "Scotso" on my headphones, tear a picture of Carlisle out of *Hit Parader* and tape it to my wall, read Mark Twain or dive for a catch onto the bed. Sometimes, being home wasn't so bad.

If I ventured out to the living room, I'd occasionally catch my father watching the news on the big piece of furniture that was the television. Sitting in his beige recliner, smoking a cigarette, me across from him on the plastic-covered pink paisley sofa, everything would aggravate my father. He'd curse at the television in Italian and proclaim how fucked-up America was. "Eh. Can you believe-a dis shitta," he'd say. "Jizzoo Greest. A-only in America. You no see-a people killa each other, stabba, shoota in-a Italy."

"Den go back to It-Lee," my mother would yell from the other room in her high-pitched Jersey City accent. "Who told ya ta move heah? For Christ's sake, awl ya do is friggin' complain. Get back on the goddamn plane a-ready."

"You shadduppa woman," he'd retort. "I tinka you do-a real-a good since I come-a to dis country…" and so on and so on until I'd calm them both down. It was a nightly ritual. My father would eventually change the channel to the Italian station, where the news was apparently less perplexing to him. I couldn't say I disagreed with him. Someone riding a scooter down a street; the Pope blessing a crowd of people; a soccer player running around the field. I didn't understand anything being said, but it definitely looked less fucked-up than, say, a guy going ballistic with a handgun on the subway, or a dog getting shot because it wouldn't stop barking.

The Pope seemed real nice.

My father might change the channel, but he knew you couldn't change the world as easily. The news from Italy might have been less disturbing and violent, but the fact remained that my father had indeed chosen to move here. Maybe that was why he always watched the American news first. Back then, there weren't a lot of choices of where to get your news. He'd watch the local and maybe one of the major network nightly news shows before switching the station. Knowing some really strange shit was going on just a few miles from where he and his family lived must have made him long for his homeland a little, and understandably. This was the world in which he lived and in which his children were growing up. This was his reality.

2 CENTERFOLD

She got up and walked quickly out of the room. She left us all there, the entire St. Nicholas second grade class, to wonder what had happened. When my teacher returned, she called me out to the hallway.

"Do you know what you have written?" she asked me. Earlier that day, we had all turned in essays on the subject of love—what it was, what we knew about it. She had been reading them. Mine was one long drawn-out analogy comparing love to a flower. This is not a groundbreaking notion, but my teacher's reaction made it seem extraordinary. "This is a very complex thing that you've done here, comparing love to a flower," she continued. My mother was called, and the essay was sent home with a long note from my teacher going on about how talented I was. It was decided right then, among my parents and siblings, that I was going to be a writer. I already loved reading, but it was at that moment that I realized that there was a person behind those words, and that perhaps I could be that person.

That I compared love to a flower should not have been surprising. One of the biggest songs of the time was "The Rose," written by Amanda McBroom and performed by Bette Midler. I was seven-years-old when that song came out, and I must have heard it frequently enough on the radio that it made an impression. There's no way, though, I could have grasped the complexity of it. The opening stanza is gut wrenching:

Some say love it is a river
That drowns the tender reed
Some say love it is a razor
That leaves your soul to bleed

This love is a far cry from any of the love—Like God's Love or Valentine's Day Love—I would have been familiar with at the time. Even now, listening back to those words, can be an emotional experience. For while Midler's delivery of the line "I say love it is a flower / and you its only seed" may appear to be positive, in the context of the impossible cruelty love is capable of in the verses, you can't be so sure.

In fourth grade, I asked my homeroom teacher if I could sing a song to the class during recess. She was happy to oblige, and at the allotted time told the class, "Listen up everyone, Joey Pagetta is going to sing a song for us."

I stepped to the front of the class in my uniform of blue pants and light blue shirt and blue plaid tie, and completely from memory sang the J. Geils Band hit, "Centerfold." If you are unfamiliar with the song, it is basically about a guy who, years after high school, is "going through a girlie magazine" and finds his "homeroom angel on the pages in between."

The song was a breakthrough hit for the J. Geils Band, and includes such classic couplets as "Slipped me notes, under the desk / While I was thinking about her dress;" "Those soft fuzzy sweaters, too magical to touch / To see her in that negligee is really just too much;" and my favorite, "Take your car, yes we will, We'll take your car and drive it / Take it to a motel room and take 'em off in private." I like that the narrator of the song didn't have his own car. As a fourth grader, I could relate.

After I sang the song, my teacher, mortified, composed herself enough to ask me in front of the other kids if I knew what the song was about. I said yes, it's about a guy who saw his girlfriend naked in a magazine. In my mind, I was probably thinking of the Sears catalog. My teacher told me it was not an appropriate song for me to listen to or sing. It was an adult song.

I don't recall it being brought up with my mother, though I'm certain they must have called her to ask what radio station I was listening to. A few weeks later I was back with another song: Queen and David Bowie's "Under Pressure."

My teacher had to approve the lyrics before I sang them, and then commended me after on both my song choice and performance. That's when I realized that lyrics such as "It's the terror in knowing what this world is about / Watching some friends screaming 'Let Me Out'" were more appropriate for a fourth grader in Catholic school than ones about naked ex-girlfriends. Buildings burning down, families splitting in two and people living on the streets was okay fodder for 10-year-old. Shaking in your shoes whenever she flashes those baby blues? Not so much.

I don't know what compelled me to get up in front of my class, unsolicited, and perform. I was an otherwise shy kid. Just a few years earlier I was locking myself in my bedroom when my uncles came to visit. But whereas in the second grade I was figuring out that there were actual people who wrote the books I was reading, by the fourth grade I had figured out that there people behind the songs, too. Performing was a way to test the waters.

I was also likely trying to impress a girl.

The first dozen songs I wrote, that same year, were part of an album I titled *Judith & Me*. By songs, I mean lyrics with melodies in my head, and by album, I mean a marble notebook, now lost to posterity. By Judith, I mean Judith, the girl in my class. I had not yet learned that you're supposed to change people's names. I even designed and sketched cover art. It featured Judith and me holding hands in a field of flowers.

Thinking back now, I've come to the conclusion that you

don't—as a fourth grader—compose an entire album's worth of songs, with cover art, because you are in love with a girl. You do it because you have figured out that words and music have the power to move people, whether it's out the door and into the hallway to the principal's office to call your mother, or to the front of the class for a teachable moment. Amanda McBroom's words and music gave Bette Midler something to sing about, which somehow gave me something to write about. Seth Justman's words and music gave The J. Geils Band one of its biggest hits and got me a talking-to by my teacher. Queen and David Bowie's words and music created one of rock's greatest collaborations, and years later gave Vanilla Ice a career. Surely I could get Judith to fall in love with me.

The funny thing is that I don't think I ever showed Judith the songs or sang them to her. And perhaps that was for the better. At that age, that I could write words and put them to melodies was probably more important than whether I could do it effectively, or as some means to an end. Everyone remembers "Centerfold," but no one knows whether the guy ever saw his homeroom angel again when her "clothes were on" just so they could "take 'em off in private." And that's how it should be.

3 ON BEING A QUEEN FAN: THE DAYS BEFORE THE DAY THAT CHANGED THE WORLD (AND THE NIGHT MY T-SHIRT LET ME DOWN)

I discovered the rock band Queen when I was nine years old. I came to them younger than most, but at the same time, later than those who knew better. Freddie Mercury, Brian May, Roger Taylor and John Deacon came to me through the airwaves of WNEW on a summer afternoon in 1980, while hanging out with my sister Mary in my brother Nick's room. I say I came to them late because in 1980, Queen had just released their album, *The Game.* "Another One Bites the Dust" was the single that I heard on the radio, and it was my first introduction to the band. While the song remains one of their biggest and most recognizable hits, anyone who knew anything about rock music at the time knew that the band's work on 1975's *A Night at the Opera,* or '74's *Sheer Heart Attack* or even 1978's *Jazz* was far superior. By the time I discovered them, they had already released a live record, 1979's *Live Killers,* a sure sign that a band had been around awhile. When I heard "Another One Bites the Dust," I jumped up on my brother's bed and started dancing.

"Who is that?" I shouted over the funky bass line to my sister.

"It's Queen," she coolly replied.

"I LOVE IT," I shouted back.

"Nicky has their album," she said and pulled the 8-track from my brother's shelf. And that was it. The combination of Mercury's soaring vocals and May's guitar solos were unlike anything I had ever heard before. I was a Queen fan. I lived and breathed the band from that point on, and had plenty of work to do. Once I absorbed *The Game*, down to knowing exactly when the 8-track would cut off mid-song, I had to track down everything else they had ever recorded.

There was a record store in the same mall in Jersey City where my Dad managed a men's clothing store and did tailoring work. So on the days I'd go to the store to help him out, I'd take my breaks at WOW Records in search of Queen music. Right off the bat, I discovered 1974's *Queen II*, a drastically different sounding record than *The Game*. While on *The Game* the band looked tough and cool in black leather framed by a blue and silver border, *Queen II* had their four faces on the cover. Their hair was longer and it looked like they were wearing make-up. The inside picture had them sitting together, very close to one another, dressed all in white. Was this the same band? The music offered further complications. The songs were full of massive choral harmonies and epic song structures, with lyrics that referenced ogres and white queens and the "Seven Seas of Rhye." What the hell were the seven seas of Rhye? Had the liner notes not stated the names of the band members, there was no way you could have convinced me this was the same band.

Despite the confusion, I loved *Queen II* just as much as *The Game*. More discovery came soon after. I bought A *Night at the Opera* on cassette, *Sheer Heart Attack* and *News of the World* on vinyl. For Christmas I asked for Queen's *Jazz* record, and freaked my family out by blasting the hymn "Mustapha" throughout the house. If that wasn't enough to disturb my parents, *Jazz* came with a poster featuring hundreds of naked women riding bicycles. At the same time that I was trying to make sense of the progression of this band that I had just become the biggest fan of, my mom and dad were surely trying to make sense of what was happening to their son. It was quite clear, though. Their son had discovered rock 'n' roll.

It wasn't easy being a Queen fan in the early 80's, especially in the Jersey City Heights. I quickly learned that among my friends who were also devouring rock 'n' roll, Queen didn't demand much respect.

"Whadda'ya a fag?" my friend Jamie asked me once.

"No," I replied. "Why?"

"Freddie's a fuckin' flamer" "

"No, he's not."

"Whadda'ya kiddin' me? Look at him. He's a fuckin' fag."

"So what?! He's da best singer in da world. Who's betta'?"

"David Lee Roth's a dousan' times betta' den Queen. AC/DC...Black Sabbath...the Stones...why don't ya' listen ta some real music, ya' fuckin' fag?"

It's true, of course, that Freddie Mercury was gay. I knew it and everyone else knew it. But I didn't care. If my friends couldn't get past it, that was their problem. They were MY band. And while they weren't as cool of a band as AC/DC or Van Halen or The Who in those peoples' eyes, I was certain they were better than all those bands combined.

But the hardest thing about being a Queen fan in the early 80's wasn't even the criticism from my friends, it was the lack of memorabilia with which to outwardly express my allegiance. There were no Queen T-shirts, or posters or hats to wear and tell the world I was a Queen fan. At the local bazaar at St. Nicholas Church, there was a booth where you could win T-shirts, and there were plenty of Iron Maiden, or Van Halen or Ozzy Osbourne, but nothing with Queen on it. I had to resort to getting a T-shirt made at an airbrush painting booth on the Jersey Shore. I somewhat designed it myself, with the name of the band, the words "A Night at the Opera," and a crown. It was great, even though the airbrush artist drew a king's crown—much like the paper Burger King ones we all remember—instead of the more bulbous queen's crown. But what did he know? He was probably a Judas Priest fan.[1]

---

[1] I was very proud of the T-shirt I designed that summer, and wore it all the time in my neighborhood, much to the good-natured abuse of my friends. I started dating Jennifer late in the summer. She was cute, a couple of years younger than me, and a gymnast. Her ex-boyfriend, Michael, was not happy about this. As far as I knew, they were broken up, which meant it was perfectly acceptable for us to share a bag a chips, or hold hands, or spit into a bottle of Coca-Cola and ask the other one to drink it to prove their affection.

Michael wanted to kick my ass. And he had a black belt in karate.

After a week of mumblings and veiled threats in the neighborhood, he confronted me. I tried my best to talk my way out of it, but by this point, with tensions high, the neighborhood kids wanted blood. My only chance at success was to throw the first punch, and with an airbrushed crown and the words "Queen" emblazoned on my chest, I felt emboldened.

I connected. The punch threw Michael backward into a car. I pounced, throwing and connecting punches recklessly to the head and body, until some of the other kids pulled me off and declared it over.

I grabbed Jennifer by the hand and walked away. I made it all away around the block — circling the neighborhood in some kind of victory lap—when a friend caught up with me. Michael wanted a rematch. Minutes later. A rematch? There were no rematches in street fights. I refused, but Michael had now assembled a gang and was determined to get his way. He wanted to meet at the local baseball field. All I could think about was the Happy Days episode where Fonzie has to fight the gang leader at the baseball park. It was ridiculous then, and even more so now. But I had no choice.

It was dark now, and with the neighborhood kids all along the outside fence, Michael and I stood in right field. I had heard that a black belt could only use their skills in self-defense, but out here, who would know? I desperately tried to talk my way out of it, knowing that this time, I truly had no chance. Oddly, Michael agreed with me.

"I just need a shot to get back at you," he pleaded. "I don't care about Jennifer."

He wasn't angry. He needed to save face, and felt I owed him an opportunity to redeem himself in front of the neighborhood. The

The 1982 release of Queen's *Hot Space* album seems to have been one of the big reasons for the lack of readily available merchandise. The album was the band's foray into music that was more disco or dance oriented, and America categorically rejected it. While it delivered the hit single "Body Language," clearly the worst song the band ever recorded, its mix of sexual innuendo and genre-busting songs only added to the public's already mixed feelings. To make matters worse, a video for the song "I Want to Break Free" featured the guys in drag. My friend Jamie had a field day with that one. It turned out that the band was mocking a British sitcom. America didn't get it.

I had what would turn out to be my only chance to see the

---

rematch was a formality.

Before I knew it was happening, he spun around and roundhouse kicked me in the face. I was down, blood gushing out of my certainly-broken nose. And so was Michael, but he wasn't on top of me finishing me off. He was apologizing to me.

"I'm so sorry," he was whispering. "I had to do it. I'm so sorry" He was using his hands to try and stop the bleeding. He was frantic.

I started laughing, almost uncontrollably. Looking back now, it's possible that I had momentarily become delirious. Or perhaps it was relief that the whole thing was over. But then I looked down and the laughing stopped.

"My shirt," I said. "My shirt. My Queen shirt has blood all over it."

"We can get a new one," Michael said."

"No, you don't understand. It's one of a kind."

He got up, knowing the charade had to continue, and walked away triumphantly. Jennifer ran to me. "Look at your boyfriend now," he said to her.

None of it was worth it. I never got the bloodstains completely out of the shirt, and while my nose wasn't broken, it was never completely straight again either. There was something romantic about the whole thing, I guess, fighting for a girl. I could say "I did it for love," like Freddie Mercury sang in "It's a Hard Life."

It's possible that Queen did let me down that night. But thinking back, I don't remember how long I dated Jennifer. Or what happened to Michael. What I do know is that you can buy Queen shirts at Target now.

band live that same year, when they visited the Brendan Byrne Arena in East Rutherford, New Jersey on the *Hot Space* tour. My friend John, who lived down the block, was older than I was and did occasional work for ticket scalpers. He told me he had a ticket to the show if I wanted to go. I begged my mother to let me go with him.

"No," she said definitively. "You're too young. They do drugs and drink at those concerts, it's not safe."

"C'mon Ma," I pleaded. "You know John. He said he'll take me and take me home. Pleeeeeaaaaaase?"

It was useless. I wasn't going. The *Hot Space* tour was the last time Queen ever toured the United States. They continued to release records throughout the 80s, but were never able to break into the American market again. America didn't want a flamboyant lead singer fronting a genre--bending band prone to sexual ambiguity, with a penchant for operatic epics, Elvis-inspired country songs and fleeting forays into funk. It didn't matter that they were the greatest rock n' roll band in the world.

My relationship to Queen had always been a personal one since I had discovered them in 1980, and after 1982, it became more so. It was as if I had to go underground with my passion and nurture it in solitude. But what was so interesting was the continuing coverage of the band in magazines like *Hit Parader* and *Creem*, which I read voraciously. There were pictures and stories about the band in Japan, the UK, and all over Europe. It looked like the band was huge everywhere else in the world but America, never mind Jersey City, New Jersey.

I continued to build my Queen music collection in my early teens, now taking the PATH train over to It's Only Rock n Roll and Revolver Records on 8th Street in Greenwich Village, New York to purchase import copies of their records and pieces of memorabilia. I longed to share this passion with others, to be in communion with other Queen fans, wherever they were. But most importantly, I longed to see them live in concert. I came close to achieving those goals one day in the summer of 1985. July 13, 1985, to be exact. The Day the Music

Changed the World.

Live Aid was the most ambitious live benefit concert event in history. Broadcast live to millions of homes throughout the world, the concert took place simultaneously at Wembley Stadium in London and JFK Stadium in Philadelphia. It brought together dozens of the world's greatest bands and artists on two stages to raise money for famine relief for the poor, starving and sick in Ethiopia. Organized by Bob Geldof—who had already done the impossible with his organizing and production of the supergroup Band-Aid and the single "Do They Know It's Christmas?"—the concert event featured The Who, Mick Jagger, Tina Turner, Bob Dylan, Black Sabbath, a young Madonna, Run DMC, Phil Collins, Paul Young, Judas Priest, George Thorogood, Elton John and more. Most importantly, it featured Queen.

On the morning of Live Aid, I woke up early to prepare myself in the living room. I set up a radio with a cassette player in order to listen to the concert simulcast on WNEW and record performances I wanted to keep. I flipped on the TV, glued myself to the recliner, and sat there for the remainder of the day, waiting for Queen's performance. There was no clear schedule as to when certain bands would be on, so I couldn't risk moving unless I was starving or in desperate need of a bathroom break. At approximately 3:44 p.m. New York time, Queen hit the stage at Wembley Stadium, forever changing my relationship to the band. And my life.

The band opened up with a bizarre move, by playing one of their biggest hits, "Bohemian Rhapsody," first. Holy shit. What kind of strange set list is this? Where can they possibly go from here? It was like they were playing their encore first! They set the bar high, and never set it down. From "Bohemian Rhapsody," they blew right into "Radio Ga Ga," inciting a sea of hands and handclaps through Wembley Stadium instantly. Here was Freddie in complete command, reaching every single person in the stadium to sing along to a song most of America could care less about. It was the most amazing testament to the power of music to move people I had ever seen, or have seen to this day. Next came "Hammer to Fall," an album cut off their 1984 album *The Works*, driven by Brian May's crunchy and melodic guitar -riff. "Crazy Little Thing Called Love" had Freddie vamping it up rockabilly-style. "We Will Rock You" and "We Are the Champions" closed the set and had an entire stadium swaying back and forth. And then it was over. I sat there dumbfounded. What did I just see? What just happened? It was like an apparition. The entire set couldn't have lasted more than 20 minutes. Had a band ever packed that much power and energy into that small amount of time? I don't think so.

I saw the power of music and performance that afternoon, and what it means to give to an audience. Freddie and the boys seemed utterly egoless that day. They had twenty minutes, and rather than start off cool and build from there, they decided to pack that time with their hits, in an almost medley--like fashion that was unrelenting. I wondered then if they also knew they had twenty minutes of prime airtime on televisions in America, and this was their chance to show them what they were missing. The band was in their prime, and for a moment I had my wish. I was watching the same thing the world was watching, at the same time. I was finally in communion with Queen fans everywhere, who no doubt were wondering if critics and naysayers were finally catching on to what we'd known all along, that Queen were indeed the greatest rock 'n' roll band in the world.

The day after Live Aid, I went around the corner to hang with the rest of the neighborhood kids on the corner where we'd play bottle caps, handball, or stick ball.

"Whe'da fuck wha' you yesterday?" Jamie asked.

"I was home watchin' Live Aid," I replied.

"You spent da whole day watchin' a fuckin' conce't on TV?"

"Yeah. Queen wha' on. Dey wha' incredible."

"Yer a fuckin' nerd. C'mon, ya in fa' stick ball?"

"Yeah. D'you pick sides yet?"

4 SPILT MILK

Growing up, there was an Irish kid in my neighborhood we called Freckle Face, but never to his actual face, mostly because we were afraid of him. Deep down, though, I knew he was all right. So when he called me Spaghetti or Spaghetti-Head it didn't really bother me that much. And he seemed to like me. He made a point of getting me out of my house, introduced me to Iron Maiden and Black Sabbath, and even told me how to make out with a girl, just before pushing me behind the stacked chairs in the gym where the girl was waiting for me. It was during the Halloween dance, and he and I were dressed up like members of Motley Crue. She was Raggedy Ann. When I asked him what to do, he shouted above the music, "Just move your fuckin' tongue around!"

I considered him a friend.

Camel Jockey, on the other hand, didn't take to his nickname very kindly, and did not think as highly of my friend as I did. One day after a touch football game in the street, incited by questionable calls, unnecessary shoves and one-too-many name calls, Camel Jockey decided he'd had enough. He waited until the moment was right, later in the day when my friend was on his way home with groceries for his mother, and jumped him right there in front of the butcher shop. We all knew it was coming, and we all knew my friend had it coming to him, but the premonition made it no less brutal. Camel Jockey exploded, leaving my friend bloody, with a broken ankle and groceries strewn all over the corner. The entire neighborhood—Dough Boy, Big Nose, Purgatory, Nigger George and me, Spaghetti-head—stood in abject horror around the scene.

My friend somehow made his way down the block to his house, and I took it upon myself to gather up his groceries. I remember being particularly sad about the busted milk carton.

My friend was in a cast and on crutches for quite a while and couldn't leave school at lunchtime. So I stayed with him most days in a vacant classroom overlooking the courtyard, eating together whatever we brought from home or whatever I went out to pick us up. We never talked about Camel Jockey, or what happened in the neighborhood. We talked about girls in our class and music and sports—the things most 12 and 13-year-olds talk about—and would occasionally fling bottle caps out the window.

After grammar school, we went on to high school together. When I got into a fight with my girlfriend's ex, my friend had my back. Literally. He was right behind me and pulled me off when it was clear I had the upper hand. When he did, he jumped on and got a few punches in himself.

It's only now, all these years later, long after we've gone our separate ways in life, that I understand my friend's actions that day. I don't think he was taking advantage of a man down. I think he was taking care of the man up. In maybe the only way he knew how.

5 WET BEHIND THE EARS

Hell hath no fury like a high school football coach scorned. I learned this valuable lesson not as a member of the coach's team—God bless those kids—but as a member of the press corps. I was 19-years-old, and recently named the youngest staff writer in the 100-plus year history of the *Jersey Journal* in Hudson County, New Jersey. I started writing for the paper two years earlier, as a paid high school intern. I covered regional Little League games, took phone calls from local softball leagues, and sometimes, very late at night, waited for the Major League Baseball box scores to come in from the West Coast so I could format them. The summer I started, the newsroom wasn't even using PageMaker software yet to design the paper, which meant column inches that were still printed and cut by hand to be laid out and photographed. It remains one of the greatest work experiences of my life.

I'm only 42 as I write this, and I can remember working in a newsroom where people came in drunk, smoked at their desks, got raging mad, and, on occasion, accused the entire editorial staff of discriminating against them because their name ended in "ski." One staff writer was a high school baseball coach who covered and wrote about other high school teams, as if this was somehow ethical. Another drank a six-pack of Coca-Cola in one sitting while pecking out stories. And then there was Leon, who looked like Marvin Gaye in the early 70s, if Gaye went to the gym five days a week and could bench press 400 pounds. This did not go unnoticed by what seemed like every black woman in Jersey City, who would call Leon at all hours.

To be 19-years-old and part of this world was an education, not only in the dysfunction of the newsroom and the world at large, but as a writer. I learned to write fast and precisely, under the pressure of hard deadlines. I came to understand that the inverted pyramid style of storytelling was not merely a suggestion, but a survival tactic. The later I turned in a story, the more likely huge chunks of the bottom of it would be sliced off. The opposite was true, as well. Young and wanting to write creatively, I would often make attempts at playing with the form. On one memorable occasion, I took two paragraphs at the beginning of my coverage of a routine Little League tournament game to draw parallels between the way Eric Clapton played guitar and the way this one particular 12-year-old pitched. My editor, Harvey, yelled from his desk,

"PAGETTA! ARE YOU FUCKIN' SERIOUS? ERIC CLAPTON? NOBODY GIVES A FUCK WHAT YOU THINK ABOUT ERIC CLAPTON! THEY WANT TO KNOW WHO WON THE GAME!"

He didn't even bother attempting to edit it. He simply lopped off the beginning two paragraphs. Fortunately, for the kids on the team and their parents, I had the winners and losers, and pitchers and hitters, in the third paragraph.

I developed a thick skin, whether it was editors tearing my work apart, or strange men in cars trying to pick me up in Journal Square as I made my way home at 2 a.m. God, I hated those West Coast games.

High school football coaches, on the other hand, were another breed of degenerate. I'm not sure I ever learned how to handle them. By the time the "youngest staff writer" designation came along, I had earned some respect as a writer and reporter. I had amassed over a hundred bylines and had written about much more than Little League. I wrote about professional football players on DUI charges, was part of conference call interviews with professional race car drivers, and could fake my way through post-game chats with college basketball coaches.

Covering football, however, was never really my thing. The sport itself held no appeal. I was a professional writer, though, and took my assignments seriously. When I was asked to cover an important St. Peter's High School football game, I grabbed my columned notebook and hit the sideline.

It was an otherwise uneventful game until early in the fourth quarter, when St. Peter's coach decided to go for a touchdown on fourth down, instead of kicking what should have been an easy field goal. This happens all the time at games. Coaches make calls and either live or die by them.

St. Peter's died by it. They lost by two points. The coach wouldn't talk to reporters after the game, so I couldn't know what he was thinking, but I imagined he was second guessing himself. Later, back at my desk at the *Jersey Journal*, that's how I wrote it. Using the operative pronoun "one" instead of "I," I started off my story with something to the effect of "In hindsight, one might look at coach so and so's decision in the fourth quarter to go for it instead of kicking a field goal as a bad decision." I—or should I say "one"—further went on to defend the coach's actions, for how was he to know, and ultimately, how was anyone to know. It's not one's place to question his decisions. There were dozens of other scenarios after that decision that could have resulted in a different outcome.

Mr. Ed Ford, whose nickname was "The Faa," was a legend in Hudson County, and his "Faa's Corner" column in the Journal was widely read. That weekend in his column, he wrote about the St. Peter's loss and referenced my questionable coverage. He referred to me as "The *Jersey Journal's* young staffer, who's still wet behind-the-ears."

I was famous. Not only did my byline appear daily in my local newspaper, but I was mentioned, in boldface type—in

Faa's Corner.

The next weekend, I was assigned St. Peter's next game. I don't recall if they won or lost, but after the game, I made my way onto the field with my notebook for the post-game interview, and when the coach saw me coming, he started screaming,

"GET HIM OUT OF HERE! GET HIM OFF THE FIELD! I'M NOT TALKING TO HIM! WHO DO YOU THINK YOU ARE QUESTIONING ME? GET HIM OFF THE FIELD."

I was being kicked off the field. For something I had written. Looking back now, it feels heroic. But then, it was embarrassing. I wanted to be respected by my fellow journalists and by the community. I was almost off the field, escorted by an assistant coach, when I heard a voice yelling, "Kid! Come back. It's all right. He'll talk to you." It was Mr. Ford, The Faa himself, the man who brought more attention to my story than I realized I needed. When I approached the coach, Mr. Ford was lecturing him. "C'mon. He didn't mean anything. Talk to him."

"Kid, he'll talk to you. "Shake hands."

And so we did. Everything was fine. I walked away with a good story and my reputation as a sports reporter intact, if a little more high profile. But I also came away with a few other things. I never used the cowardly word "one" as a pronoun in a story again. I saved that for when had my own sports column in my college newspaper—"Time Out with Joe Pagetta."

My other takeaway: high school football coaches may think they're more important than they are, but sometimes, so do local sports reporters.

6 WHEN PRESS BEAT DEPRESSION

At 18 years old, I wrote a letter to a local music reporter and told her about my band. It was a rash decision, done without much thought. I figured if I could tell someone about me, and about my band, I could break free. Of what, exactly, I wasn't sure. Maybe my bedroom. Maybe myself.

We were a good band that worked hard. We practiced five nights a week, played a lot of local shows, and took ourselves more seriously than 18-year-olds ever should. We had a live demo that kicked ass and was surely better than anything coming out of Hudson County in those days. Better yet, at the beginning of the 1990s, Horror Time was easily the best band in northeast New Jersey. We knew it. The only problem was that no one else did. No one knew we even existed. That meant, of course, no one knew I existed.

So, late on this night, I sat down and wrote Cathie Coleman at the *East Coast Rocker* a long drawn-out letter introducing myself and my band and explaining how we could really use some press. It was that simple. We weren't getting anywhere and weren't really sure where we were trying to go. We didn't fit in with Bon Jovi or Skid Row or, God forbid, any of the hair metal bands popular on the radio and in the area. We weren't heavy enough to run with the hardcore bands selling out matinees in New York or speaking for the angst of the kids in the suburbs of New Jersey. But then again, we weren't a Jersey rock band like the E Street Band or the Asbury Jukes, either. We kind of thought of ourselves as a thing and style all our own. We were an attitude and a philosophy. Four kids (three Italian Americans and one Indian American) on a mission to take over the world with six-to-seven-minute songs (at least!) and a heavy dose of influence from The Misfits, The Ramones, Gorilla Biscuits, Supertouch, Vision, Metallica, and early U2. A strange mix of bands you've heard of and some you haven't. You were going to hear about us.

First, we had to get out of Jersey City.

I took our live demo, my letter, a bio a friend had written, and a grainy photo, and put it all in a golden padded envelope. The next morning, I walked the ten or so blocks up to the post office on Central Ave near Grand Street in the Heights.

I didn't know anything about follow-up calls, so I wouldn't be sure if Coleman ever got the package. There was no email to do a follow-up email, and no internet, where I might have been able to check the magazine's website. I would just have to pick up the East Coast Rocker every Thursday and see if we were in there.

My hopes weren't high. As far as I knew, bands didn't get written about because band members wrote letters to music writers. There was some mystery involved in the whole process, I was sure. I used to make frequent trips up to Garden State News on the corner of Bauer Street and Central Avenue, not far from the post office, to pick up copies of *Creem* and *Hit Parader*. All the bands; all the stories. The magazines must have known about these people and sought them out for interviews and features. When you're great, I figured, magazines knew who you were.

In the weeks that followed my gutsy mailing maneuver, it was back to the routine. School, work, late night band practice, and fighting depression in my bedroom on the appropriately named Booraem (pronounced bore-em) Avenue in Jersey City Heights.

It was a dark bedroom. Enclosed by dusty gray paneling and anchored by forest-green wall-to-wall carpeting, it had one window that faced the alleyway between our house and Angelo and Hazel's house next door. There was no natural light. Occasionally, the smell of cat urine would waft over from Angelo and Hazel's, who shared their house with at least 17 cats. Exactly how many cats they had was hard to calculate. Your best shot was to keep track of which ones were sitting in their front window and make a mental note of which ones you hadn't seen before.

I moved into the room about a year earlier, after my family had moved apartments from the second floor to the first. The first floor was most recently occupied by my grandmother; before that, by both my grandmother and grandfather; and before that by my grandmother, grandfather, my mother, and her two brothers. There was a lot of history in that apartment. My grandmother had been living in it by herself for the last nine years, after the death of my grandfather in December of 1980.

When my grandmother died in 1989, she'd been in a nursing home for only a few days. For the many months before that, she'd lain in a hospital bed that had been placed in the living room. My mother, with occasional help from me and my sister and brother, cared for her—emptying her bed pan, rolling her over to prevent bed sores, and giving her sponge baths. After her death, my parents decided it was best for us to move down to the first floor and rent out the second. My parents took the master bedroom, my sister, Mary, took my Uncle Vinnie's old room closest to the kitchen, and I took my Uncle Joe's old room off the living room where my grandmother spent her last months. My brother claimed the basement, which meant the rest of us lost unrestricted access to it and needed his approval to wash our clothes.

It took a little over a month of trips to the newsstand on Central Avenue before I finally found out if Coleman ever got my letter and package. She did. There in her "New Jersey Newsbeat" column was Horror Time, looking tougher and more rock 'n' roll than ever. We were the second item. She wrote a few paragraphs about us, telling folks that we were a band to look out for. She even quoted a few lines from our bio, and made a point to mention how young we were, even referring to us as a "baby band" in line with early 90s hit makers, and coincidentally Jersey-based, Trixter.

The band was ecstatic. We were on the map. People knew who Horror Time was. It seemed like everyone saw the article, and for those who didn't, there was sure to be a copy in each band member's back pocket if necessary. I realized quickly that press could breed more press. And now that I knew you could be directly responsible for getting your band in the papers, I jumped on the opportunity to get us more. I was able to garner listings mentions, reviews, and show previews in some of the other local newspapers, like *The Jersey Journal* and *The Hudson Current*. When Horror Time put out its first proper demo, I sent Cathie Coleman a copy. She wrote about us in her column again, and this time we were the lead item.

Many of my band's friends and contemporaries, when reading stories about us, frequently asked, "How'd you get that?" My answer was always the same: "I sent them some stuff."

I realized that most people thought getting press was as mysterious as I once did. But now I knew it wasn't. You had to let the press know about you. In the years that followed, through Horror Time's demise and the building of my own singer-songwriter career, I gathered a decent collection of press clippings about my music in both regional and national publications. I learned how to write a professional press release and bio, how to write cover letters, and how to get professional promo photos taken. I built press and contact lists, and learned about something I didn't know existed when I was 18 and in my first band: the follow-up.

I never again wrote a late-night, depression-fueled plea to a music writer to tell him or her about my band, although I sometimes wish I was still innocent enough to think doing so is appropriate.

It wasn't long after that first bit of press that my family moved from Booraem Avenue, forced out by uncles who wouldn't accept my parents' offer to buy out their share of my grandmother's estate. At the same time we were preparing to find another place to live, my mother decided she wanted a divorce from my father after 25 years of marriage. Dealing with the illness and death of my grandmother, and the realization that her two brothers would just as soon put her out on the street, was too much for a woman who I know now was struggling with an undiagnosed delusional disorder. And then there was my father's gambling addiction and chronic misery, magnified by the circumstances and impossible for anyone to handle. We all needed to come together. Instead, we fell apart.

I couldn't afford to live on my own at the time, so I popped back and forth. I lived a few months with my mother, then after she got tired of me, a few months with my father. It was a vagabond, pack-light existence, where I frequently slept at my girlfriend's house, and on one occasion when both of her parents were drunk and vicious, in my car, parked in the covered garage under my father's apartment building. None of that mattered, though. I was out of that dark and depressing bedroom off the living room. And I was on my way. More shows.[2] More press. More existence outside of myself.

---

[2] It was—at the time—the most important gig of my life. Early-to-mid 90s. The Bitter End on Bleecker Street in New York City. The place where the legends played. I earned it in a roundabout way. A friend who studied with the same vocal teacher as me couldn't play his show, so he convinced Kenny Gorka, the Bitter End's booking agent, that I could fill his slot. It wasn't the best night, a Sunday, and not the best time, around 11 p.m., but the Bitter End was always good for a tourist crowd and walk-in traffic. I was 21, and after some years of playing as part of a band, was striking out on my own as a singer-songwriter with my own band. My bass player couldn't make it for some reason, and my drummer, who was 16, couldn't get the go-ahead from his parents to make the trek from New Jersey into New York on a school night. I'd have to go it solo.

I was terrible.

I forgot lyrics. Flubbed guitar parts. And in a particularly emotive moment, guitar slung low, head down and creeping back toward the front of the stage like a true artist, slammed my head into the microphone, creating a loud thump and almost knocking the mic and stand off the stage. The most important gig of my life turned into the worst gig of my life.

My friend called me the next day.

"Joe, what the hell happened last night? Kenny's pissed at me for recommending you. He said you were terrible and couldn't touch you for a few months."

I tried to explain, but knew the only solution was to redeem myself. I called and begged Kenny to give me another shot. He reluctantly offered me another gig. A couple of months later, on a random weekday night, with the full Joe Pagetta Band in tow, I returned to the Bitter End and kicked ass.

Kenny loved us and called me the next day to ask us back in a few weeks. We continued to do this, working our way toward a coveted weekend slot. At the Bitter End, though, redemption was never guaranteed. At least two more times, Kenny threatened to never book us again.

There was one time when we invited a keyboard player and soon-to-be-band-member to sit in with us on the house piano. The result was a mess. Paul, who was Kenny's right-hand man and eyes and ears, was furious when we got off the stage.

"Joe, what the hell was that? You sounded terrible. This is the Bitter End. We have a reputation to uphold. You wanna pull that shit, go around the corner to (lower east side club) the Orange Bear. Now go back to fuckin' New Jersey and practice."

I called Kenny the next day to book our next gig. "Joe, I can't touch you. I heard you brought up a piano player and it sounded like shit." We rehearsed with our new keyboard player, and returned, triumphantly, once again. It went on this like. Getting it right, getting it wrong. But always redemption.

Except for maybe that one time Kenny found out we played at another club on Bleecker, a block or so away. It lacked the history and respect of the Bitter End, but we were desperate to play anywhere and anytime.

"Joe, did you play down the street?" Kenny asked the next time I called him. "I can't touch you for three months if you play there. It makes us look band. That place is for amateurs."

One day, during one of the brief stints I lived with my father on Sherman Avenue in Jersey City, the *Jersey Journal* sent over a photographer to take a few photos of me. I had won a singer-songwriter competition at the Village Gate in Greenwich Village, and in addition to the fifty dollars I received, I was given a showcase of my own at the club. I tipped the *Journal* off about the competition and show, and it decided to do a little piece on me, with an accompanying photo. The photographer took a few shots, and the paper ran the one of me sitting with my guitar propped up in front of me—the standard "musician who plays guitar" shot. But there was another photo taken, that the photographer gave me later, which I've always felt captured that time in my life quite accurately. In it I was holding a lit cigarette and standing by the window, looking outside myself and my father's apartment, toward a world that was beginning to know I existed. I had the photo and the story in the paper to prove it.

I begged for forgiveness, but I was also nearing the end of my need for redemption and plotting my move to Nashville. I don't recall if we ever played the Bitter End after that. I called Kenny once years later. I was now living in Nashville and putting together a Northeast tour. I wanted to include a stop at the Bitter End. We couldn't find the right date, but he remembered me and was kind.

The best thing about those years, and the on-again off-again relationship with Kenny and the Bitter End, was that he never once talked to me about draw. Return engagements had nothing to do with how many people we brought out to see us, or what the bar take was. It was always about how good we were and how well we played. Anyone who's ever played in a band that worked bars and clubs knows how rare that is, and important it can be in your development. In his own cantankerous, but always caring, way, Kenny made me a better musician and performer. For that, I and the thousands of other musicians he gave gigs to, will always be thankful.

Kenny Gorka died on March 19, 2015, in New York City. He was 68.

JOE PAGETTA

7 GOING AWAY EGGPLANT

It was to be my farewell dinner. I'd be moving to Nashville later that week and my family thought it'd be a good idea to all get together at my sister's house. My brother even showed up, and he never showed up for anything.

My nephew Joey, my sister's second child, was born a few weeks earlier, and my sister kept storming through the kitchen and onto the deck so fast to smoke that the dozen or so times she did it seemed like déjà vu each time it happened. By the end of the day, I was convinced she had only had one cigarette. She'd held off for nine months and figured she had every right to start again with gusto. Who was I to argue?

My father had decided to make stuffed eggplant, since he knew it was my favorite dish. For at least one day, the kitchen was like the kitchen of my youth on Sunday mornings, when I'd awake to the sound and smell of sautéed garlic sizzling in olive oil, preparing itself for the waterfall of crushed tomatoes soon to arrive. It was a fitting aroma to accompany a last family dinner before my departure to a town where homemade Italian cooking was sure to be scarce.

I sat outside most of the late morning and afternoon with my girlfriend, simultaneously soaking it all in while letting it all go. It was goodbye to New Jersey, and goodbye to my brother, whom I'd probably see as much when I moved 900 miles away as I did then, when he lived about twenty.

My family didn't really get together like this on Sundays anymore, at least not like we did years ago when my grandfather was still alive. We'd eat at 1:00 every Sunday afternoon after mass, down in the finished basement of the house we shared. Surrounded by wood paneling, we connected a few tables, covered them with a vinyl red-and-white checked tablecloth, and sat down to mounds of pasta, meats, breads, salads, jugs of Gallo table wine, 7up for the kids and plenty of beautiful noise.

We were older now, with many complicated lives that occasionally crossed paths if an opportunity presented itself. I was glad to be that opportunity.

Dinner was almost ready when my brother threw open the sliding kitchen door that led to the deck and pronounced loudly to everyone on the deck (and the neighborhood) that he was leaving.

"I'm leaving," he declared.

"Whattaya mean, you're leaving," I inquired.

"John Edward just hit Joey and she's not doing anything about it and I can't take this shit anymore."

"Nicky, just calm down," my mother chimed in, distracted from her pleasant conversation with me and my girlfriend regarding our housing, employment and creative plans once we got to Nashville.

"No," he shouted back. "He's gonna hurt that baby."

My father, who was standing over the stove, behind my brother in the kitchen, took off his pot holder gloves, mumbled something in Italian and tried to quell the situation. It doesn't matter what he said to my brother, because it didn't work. It didn't work, because nothing would have worked. He didn't want to be there and this was his out.

Had John Edward not hit Joey, which, as it turns out, he didn't—he merely tried to hug his new younger brother a little less gently than he should have, as toddlers often do—it wouldn't have mattered.

The simple fact that he showed up in his dark-blue Dickies-designed air-conditioning repairman outfit, claiming he was on call and might have to run if there was an emergency, indicated that he didn't plan on staying very long. He could've told his boss that he needed the day off, that his little brother was moving to Nashville, the first of his family to break out of New Jersey. But he didn't.

He slammed the sliding door shut, walked through the kitchen, into the dining room, descended the three steps into the living room, proceeded straight through into the vestibule, out the front door, across the lawn, got into his air-conditioning repairman truck, started it and drove away. Or at least I imagine that's the path he took and order in which it happened, since that was the only way it could have happened. I imagine it because I didn't get up from my spot on the deck to stop him or to follow him out, too stunned to move or accept that he was actually leaving like that, without even saying goodbye to his little brother. Without even giving him a hug or a handshake.

And without even a taste of my father's stuffed eggplant, which was sure to be his best yet. What kind of person walks out on eggplant?

8 WHERE WERE YOU?

On the morning of Tuesday, Sept. 11, 2001, I was laid out on the living room couch of my fiancé Kathy's East Nashville home, drugged up on antibiotics and steroids and preparing to take the day off. We were supposed to get married in four days, and I was fighting off my annual sinus infection. I remember her waking me up by turning the television on and telling me that a plane had crashed into one of the towers. I was in a fog and wasn't sure what I was watching, but then we both sat in horror, with the rest of the world, as the second plane hit, and then the towers fell. It was all surreal, of course, and the hours after were inconceivable. She went to work, and we kept in constant contact the rest of the day as the story unfolded.

I grew up looking at the Towers from my Jersey City Heights home, and I'd worked for a couple of years in Tower One of the World Trade Center, on the 67th and 68th floors, starting just months after the first bombing in 1993. On 9/11, I worried about the people I knew at the Port Authority and all the friends I had in New York. Information about them was scarce, and I remember talking with my best friend Kevin's girlfriend, Jolee, several times during the day. Kevin was to be my best man, and he worked in New York City. His girlfriend was near hysterical on the phone, unable to locate him. There was nothing I could do but comfort her and hope to hear from him. I did eventually, much later that night. He had walked home, like many bridge-and-tunnellers.

My friend Tom called me later in the day to remind me that my bachelor party was that night. I had completely forgotten, and now aware of it, told him I really didn't want to do anything. He suggested we at least get something to eat. So he and his sons Thomas and Paul—my extended family, really—went to Ruth's Chris Steak House. We barely ate and were glued to the news on the television like everyone else. They asked if I wanted to go the strip club (oddly enough, Deja Vu was open) but I just wanted to go home. Thomas had a suggestion: Why don't we go down the block to what I think was a Blockbuster music store at the time, and everyone buy me a used CD? So that's what we did. I got Darden Smith's *Deep Fantastic Blue*, Bruce Springsteen's *Live in New York City*, and something else I don't remember, and that was my bachelor party. Later that night, sitting on the front porch, smoking a cigarette, Kathy came home from her own bachelorette party, and both of us commiserated about our nights, and the ridiculousness of having gone through with them at all.

The next day, there were decisions to be made. Planes were grounded for the foreseeable future, and my entire family and best man were up in the New York area. The idea of celebrating anything seemed inappropriate. We considered postponing the wedding, but everyone we called said unequivocally that we must go through with it. So we did, and people rallied around us. My family, including my divorced parents, my sister and brother-in-law (soon to be divorced themselves), and their young sons all piled into a van to make the drive from New Jersey to Nashville. Kevin left Jersey City at midnight Thursday night/Friday morning to drive to Philadelphia and meet up with another friend he had never met, to make the drive down. Kathy's family all drove in from Missouri, and her sister brought us a huge antique American flag to drape off our roof. We had the rehearsal dinner that Friday night at Kathy's house, complete with Whitt's Barbecue and my soon-to-be mother-in-law's legendary cheese grits, and it was beautiful.

Kevin was bummed that I didn't have a proper bachelor party and insisted we go out that night. We didn't get far. The stress of the week, including being trapped in New York City for hours and unable to get back to New Jersey, had finally gotten to him. In the parking lot of our first stop, he completely broke down. So there I was, the night before my wedding, comforting my best friend and best man.

The wedding and reception were a celebration of the highest order. I had originally told our DJ that I didn't want any silly songs, no "Chicken Dance" or "YMCA" or "Electric Slide," but there I was, using whatever prop was handed to me, dancing and singing and being the silliest one at the party. The reception ended as all good New York/New Jersey weddings (and Yankees home games) should, even though we were in Nashville, even though the world we knew had been shattered four days ago, with Frank Sinatra's "New York, New York." We sang it louder than ever, shouting it to the heavens, less in celebration than in collective prayer. To this day, people still tell me it was the best wedding they've ever attended. It was a celebration of life, like a big, boisterous, alcohol and food-fueled reception following a funeral.

Our honeymoon plans included a trip to Cancun on the morning after our wedding, and as of the afternoon of the wedding, with planes still grounded, we still weren't sure we were going anywhere. But the airports opened up, and early the next morning we hustled to Nashville's airport to catch our mostly-deserted flight to mostly-deserted Cancun. In Mexico we met a gorgeous young Israeli couple, also on their honeymoon. They empathized with us, and the American people, in a way I guess only they could. They lived every day in the heightened state that we soon would. But they believed in living life, and not letting fear control them, and told us so. And I guess so did we, but only because in a few short days, we had seen and felt the worst and best: The horror and the humanity of that day, quickly balanced by the conviction and perseverance of the people around us who loved us and refused to let anything get in their way. For Kathy and me, it was a strange, and yet strangely beautiful, way to begin a new life.

9 MUSSOLINI AND ME

I'm not sure how or when it happened, but at some point, I became the keeper of my family's photo archive. It started in a suitcase, and now resides in a flimsy aluminum lock box. Every now and then, on the hunt for a photo to mark a special occasion like a significant birthday or a Throwback Thursday on social media, I rummage through it and consider organizing it. I rarely get further than stuffing photos into an envelope marked "me."

There are snapshots of family vacations in the Poconos (my sister and I dressed alike); great photos of my mother's strange hairstyles and colors; plenty of people I don't know and don't want to know; and a fairly impressive visual timeline of my father going from an eternally cool and handsome guy in the 50s and 60s, with close-cropped hair, Ray Ban sunglasses and a style to rival Marcello Mastroianni in Fellini's *La Dolce Vita*, to someone who looks exactly like the 1970s and 80s, with a gut, longer hair parted on the side with sideburns, and tinted eyeglasses. Think Al Pacino in *Donnie Brasco*. I'm not sure how that happened, either.

There is also a wallet-sized, black-and-white photo of Benito Mussolini. I think I know how that happened. The fascist Italian dictator has been a part of my family for a long time.

My father was an Italian immigrant who came to the United States in the early 1960s. He met my mother, a second generation Italian American, they got married, and by the late 1960s, they'd settled down in Jersey City, New Jersey and started a family. I was the youngest of three. We didn't have a communal family library in the apartment where we lived, on the second floor above my mother's parents, but we did have a book about Mussolini that sat on a shelf in the hutch – we called it a "china cabinet" – in the dining room. In 1985, when I was in my early teens, my whole family gathered around the living room TV to watch the miniseries, *Mussolini: The Untold Story*, starring George C. Scott as the dictator. It was a big event for my father, on par with my mother's excitement over *The Thorn Birds* three years earlier. George C. Scott was no Richard Chamberlain, but he was handsome in his own way.

In the club where my father played cards with friends from the old country, there was a portrait of Mussolini hanging proudly above one of the tables.

I didn't know much about Mussolini from my school history classes. Fascist; aligned with Hitler; part of the Axis powers, shot and killed by his own people and hanged upside down along with his mistress. That was about it. He was an evil guy, clearly. But here was my father, who seemed to love this guy for no good reason that I or my brother or sister could figure out. He expressed no anti-Semitism or homophobia, outside of the stereotypical tropes that were common back then. His boss was Jewish, and they had a good friendship. They sometimes took their wives out together on a double date. The guy who dressed the windows at the store where my father worked was gay. Other than referring to him as a "finocchio," the Italian word for fennel — he pronounced it "finewk" — he otherwise didn't seem to care. He also referred to black people occasionally as "moolinyahns," his pronunciation of "melanzane," the Italian word for eggplant. I'm not sure why Italians use vegetables as derogatory terms, especially since they don't make sense. Eggplant is purple. Fennel is, I don't know, excellent when paired with mandarin oranges in a salad with a little bit of olive oil.

My father's love of Mussolini wasn't something any of us really worried about. It was humorous, even. When my father eventually got a desktop computer in the late 90s and discovered you could set up a picture of your own choosing as wallpaper, he asked me and my sister to make it Mussolini. Sure thing, Pop.

This is not to say that my father was a perfect man with a weird fascination with Mussolini. Those evenings he spent at the Italian club playing cards sometimes turned into entire weekends in Atlantic City without advance notice, leaving my mother crying and cursing his name. Weekends in Atlantic City turned into massive debts to casinos that drained the family's savings. He could also be verbally and physically abusive. One of my most vivid memories is of him throwing a two-liter bottle of soda at my mother. It was 7Up, because that was all we drank. We were in the basement, in the furnace room area. I don't know what they were arguing about or why we were in there. It might have been where we kept the extra stock of soda. It hit her right in the chest. I have this other memory of when I was a little older and in my teens, of waking up with his hands around my neck. I don't remember what he was angry about—it was the morning after a night of losing at the club— but he got off me and made a move for an acoustic guitar that I had propped up in my bedroom. I jumped out of bed and started screaming and threatening him until he left. Sometimes when I think about this second memory, I wonder if it's true. I sounds like too good of an origin story for someone who went on to become a musician, especially when I think of another time when I was a bit younger and my father helped me repair a cheap Cort-brand Flying V electric guitar. The electronics connecting the pickups had separated, so we set the guitar up on the kitchen table and he showed me how to use a soldering gun. I'm not sure I trust that story either.

In 2000, spurred on by the death of one of his brothers,

and my encouragement, my father and I took a trip together back to Italy. Considering our tumultuous history, it was risky. But I was no longer a child or even a teenager. I was a 28-year-old man open to reconciliation and in search of a connection to my heritage. Before heading south to his homeland, we decided to fly into Milan and take trains down through all the major cities. Everywhere we went, my father had to point out to me the significant landmarks connected to Mussolini. Milan was a good place to start. There is, of course, the Milano Centrale train station, rebuilt and inaugurated by Mussolini's regime in 1931. There is the visage of Mussolini, along with Vittorio Emanuele II, on one of the spires of the Cathedral in Milan. There are numerous and remarkable Fascist-era buildings all over the city. And then there is Piazza Loreto, where the bodies of Mussolini and his mistress, Clara, were dumped and then hanged upside down to be stoned and beaten with sticks. My father was determined to pay his respects at this location, and not only made me figure out how to get there from our hotel, but made me go into a cafe to ask a barista where exactly it happened. There was no marker,; and to my father's dismay, no monument. My father even requested that I take a picture of him on the spot.

While I found this whole adventure slightly macabre, if amusing, I appreciated my father's childlike enthusiasm. He was me visiting the corner of E Street and 10th Avenue in Belmar, New Jersey, where Bruce Springsteen and the E Street Band rehearsed; or me in Montgomery, Alabama at the F. Scott Fitzgerald House. Only instead of wanting to be close to a storied musician or author, he was communing with a dead fascist dictator.

But by the time we got to Venice, I had had enough. In a journal I kept at the time, there is this entry, dated September 12, 2000:

"We nap and then head out again for coffee and discover a gallery that houses works by Dalí. Entry is expensive, but I browse the store with lithographs of Dalí, as well as plates and other ceramics designed by

Picasso. Very cool. My father couldn't give a shit. Seems the only thing he gives a shit about is Mussolini. That's the only time he gets passionate. With a couple of Pellegrinos and some smokes, we sit awhile at Piazza San Marco and talk about WWII and fascism and socialism and Mussolini and Germany."

It's during that conversation that my father finally laid out his theory on Mussolini, which begins with his father, my grandfather, fighting in the Italian army when it invaded Ethiopia (then Abyssinia) in 1935. My father was one year old. Mussolini justified that invasion in plenty of ways, including the gathering of resources during the Great Depression and finding work for unemployed Italians. It was in Ethiopia that my grandfather contracted malaria, an infection that my father believed was connected to the leukemia that eventually killed him. With that as context — whether he intentionally set it up that way or not — my father went on to paint a picture of Mussolini as someone who truly cared about the Italian people, and as someone who considered Italian Jews nothing less than Italians and did not agree with Hitler's anti-Semitic views. My father believed that Italy only aligned with Germany because if it hadn't, the Third Reich would have rolled over Italy like it had Poland. The army was weak from the war in Ethiopia, after all. My father basically considered Mussolini a good guy who got mixed up with the wrong people.

This is an abridged and over-simplified version of that conversation. It's been awhile since my father and I took that trip, and more than a decade since he died. The veracity of his claims about Mussolini doesn't matter. There is plenty of material out there to support or disprove them. What matters is that I didn't try to change his mind. I listened. I didn't suggest that the invasion of Ethiopia was an act of aggression, and that Italy used chemical weapons. I didn't present another view of Mussolini as a demagogue who preyed on the Italian peoples poverty with promises of greatness and a return to its Roman Empire glory days. We were not in history class. He and I were not on opposing debate teams. We were a father and a son with a couple of cigarettes by a thousand-year-old fountain in Piazza San Marco having a conversation I'd wanted to have my entire life. My father was telling me his story.

In retrospect, the context my father provided offered a clue to his thought process. My grandfather would have believed his work in the Italian army to be noble. It's not hard to see how that might have been passed down to my father, a kid growing up poor in the south of Italy during the Great Depression and into the second World War. Considering my grandfather's eventual death, it's easy then, too, to see how my father would have not wanted his father's death to be in vain.

After our conversation, there were a few more Mussolini-themed events once we got to his hometown, including an illicit conversation in the doorway of a nondescript building, followed by a walk down the block and a return to that doorway fifteen minutes later, to retrieve an 8"x10" photo of my father's favorite dictator.

Set in Italy, there's a scene in Luca Guadagnino's 2017 film, *Call Me By Your Name*, when the characters and lovers Elio and Oliver stop at a stranger's house to ask for a glass of water. Oliver notices an image of Mussolini above the doorway. "Il Duce," he says. "That's Italy," Elio responds, matter-of-factly. Not knowing better in 2000, I would have responded the same way.

The trip was worth the risk. My father and I became friends after it, because, I think, neither of us tried to change the other or the past. We met each other where we were, and found something to connect to and be proud of. We understood each other.

We didn't talk about Mussolini much in the seven years before he died, and I hadn't really thought about the dictator much until I found that photo in my box. It was weird, but also made me smile.

I miss my father. I wish he was here to meet my twin daughters, one of whom is named after his brother, Pinuccio, whose death was the reason we went to Italy in the first place.

I don't have a picture of Mussolini on my laptop, nor is there a picture of Mussolini hanging in any of the places I hang out with my friends. There are no books about him in my home library. And in my many subsequent trips back to Italy since my father's death, I haven't visited any of his favorite Mussolini landmarks. That was his history, not mine. My history is this story.

10 SLEEPING ON COUCHES

For some people, memories of nights spent on couches are badges of honor, souvenirs of a hitchhiking trip across America or partying all night and crashing at a friend's apartment. For others, they're battle scars, emblems of yet another marital war. "Yeah," you hear them say, as if they'd taken a bullet for a comrade. "Slept on the couch that night."

Aspiring musicians tend to maintain the most sentimental remembrances of sleeping on couches, crisscrossing the country from one dive bar or coffee house to another, counting on the kindness of strangers for a warm meal and a blanket in the living room. I was a singer-songwriter in my previous life, or at least what feels like another era, but I have no romantic tales of couch time on the road. Not because the bookings failed to come, or the records failed to sell, but because I couldn't do it. I had spent too much time without a home, crashing wherever I could, and nothing about it was romantic.

I was nineteen when my parents divorced, and with the dissolution of their marriage came the selling of the family house in Jersey City. I wasn't young, but I wasn't old enough to live on my own, either. Commuting to college and working to pay for tuition, I couldn't afford my own place. My parents each rented a one-bedroom apartment in the city, and at first I went to live with my mother and her Victorian-style, plastic-covered couch. But it was she who had filed for divorce, who had wanted out of the marriage, and it was clear she wanted to be alone. After a few months, I moved in with my father, whose apartment was in a fairly new building conveniently located down the block from the club where he liked to play cards. A pimp occupied the penthouse apartment, and every night there'd be different women climbing or descending the stairs. This arrangement was problematic only once—the time my car got towed. It was registered to the address where both my father and the pimp lived, and, putting two and two together, the cops accused me of being the pimp. I tried to convince them I was a college student. When they asked me if I had anything to do with the "ladies down there," I thought they were talking about Margie in the financial aid office. How my Datsun 280ZX wasn't proof I wasn't a pimp is beyond me.

My father didn't want the divorce, and everything about the situation made him bitter. He was miserable, and he would start arguments and then kick me out. Many mornings I would lie on the cardboard-colored couch that came with the apartment and pretend to be sleeping until he left for work, just to avoid dealing with him. I was missing a lot of my early classes, though, so I went back to live with my mother. It wasn't long until she, too, kicked me out. I moved back in with my father, who now made a daily ritual of kicking me out. I slept at my girlfriend's house sometimes, but her mother and stepfather were alcoholics. One time she and I both slept in the Datsun, parked in the underground garage of my father's building.

Fed up and feeling a bit homeless, I called up my older brother, who lived in the suburbs, and asked if I could live with him. After all, he had a couch.

At first we got along fine, but he was going through his own brand of misery involving a married woman. Already a cigarette smoker, I took up cigars and a pipe, just to justify spending all my time outside in the courtyard. Smoking may be bad for you, but it's a great excuse when you need to walk away from something. Finally, about a year later, my father called and said he'd found a two-bedroom apartment, one with a basement apartment attached, and asked both my brother and me to move back to Jersey City to live with him. By this time, I was nearing the end of college, and my goal was clear: graduate, find a full-time job, and get my own place.

Within a year I had done it; I was out. I had spent close to four years living on couches, but those days were over. I had a bed of my own, and I bought a chartreuse-green couch with a pull-out bed from the Salvation Army, just in case a friend needed a place to stay. For a while, a musician friend did.

Through it all, I was playing my songs all over New Jersey and New York. When I was twenty-six, I moved to Nashville to try to make a living with music. I took a full-time job and worked a part-time job, too, to make ends meet. I met a woman at work and fell in love. Three years later, I was married. I continued to play and write songs, sometimes with my wife, and put out a few independent records that got some attention. In 2005, I released a record with some of Nashville's finest musicians and a few guest singers. It was the closest thing I had to a breakthrough. There was critical acclaim, in the states and overseas, healthy airplay on college radio throughout the country, and gigs that actually paid. After months of discussion, my wife and I agreed that the time was ripe to give music a proper shot. And so I hit the road, playing gigs in Boston, New York, Philadelphia, D.C.

My life on the road didn't last long. About a year later, I woke up on a fellow musician's couch in Cambridge, Massachusetts, and I realized I couldn't do it. I wasn't hung over. The gig the night before wasn't particularly good or bad. Nothing significant had happened. I simply accepted that after working so hard to make something of myself, I couldn't spend any more time sleeping on other people's couches. It's a game you have to play if you want to sleep, someday, on tour buses or in hotel rooms, and I realized I didn't want to play the game. I didn't want it enough. I missed my wife. I missed my bed.

So I stopped touring, and then I stopped taking even the local gigs. I felt paralyzed. My dream had collapsed around me, and I needed to rethink everything I thought I wanted to do, everything I wanted to be. Forging a new self takes a while. I managed it, in time. My marriage, however, already struggling, suffered.

In 2011, my wife and I separated. I rent a house now in West Nashville, with a bedroom and a small office, and I have the beat-up leather furniture my wife didn't want. There are nights when the loneliness is too much for me, and I find myself sleeping on the couch. But this time it's strangely comforting, reminiscent of a time in transition, when the couch is merely a stop on a journey toward something more permanent, and more my own.

11 TWO WHEELS AND THE TRUTH

Knowing I'd be holding baby Sophia in a few short miles made the strenuous, blind-curve, no-shoulder climb going north over Backbone Ridge that much easier. It's never been entirely easy. I remember the first time I tried to do it, five years ago. I couldn't. I stopped halfway up and sat on a guardrail, gasping for air, my chest tight. But that was before I was diagnosed with asthma, back when I thought sixteen years of smoking had done irreparable damage to my lungs. Now, cigarettes years behind me, asthma in check, and my lungs and legs healthier and stronger, I take bigger breaths, climb in larger gears on larger hills, and, on this occasion, think about holding babies.

The chilly spring was fading, which made my ride from the Belle Meade area of Nashville southeast to the town center of Franklin perfect for my customary mid-ride mocha at the coffee shop. Most area cyclists know a good part of this route. The stretch of Old Natchez Trace along the Harpeth River, although peaceful and pastoral, can be miserable on a bike, because the city of Franklin or the county of Williamson or whoever is responsible for these things, can't seem to get around to paving it. But it dumps you out onto Del Rio Pike, which is straightway-flat heaven. You zip by horses and cows—cows tend to follow you with their heads—and old farms and big houses. I grew up in the city and have no idea why this is so pleasant to me. Come to think of it, I didn't grow up an athlete either and have no idea why I've taken so hard to wearing really tight and colorful spandex clothing while riding a bicycle that is worth more than my car. (Which doesn't necessarily mean anything: I own a 2001 Suzuki Esteem with almost 100,000 miles on it.) But that's as it should be, as my bike-riding friends remind me.

Sophia's dad, my close friend Thomas, had texted me mid-mocha to ask if I still wanted the beat-up, in-need-of-serious-restoration, '50s dinette set he had been holding for me. I didn't. You know how you think you're a certain kind of person who likes a certain kind of thing, but then you get to a certain age and have to accept that maybe you are not that person? I used to think I was a '50s dinette kind of person. I'm not. Or I'm not anymore. But then Thomas asked if I wanted to stop by anyway to see him and Becki and Sophia. Of course I did.

The dinette set, along with an array of other things Thomas and Becki didn't know what to do with, was outside the garage. Inside with her parents was Sophia, ten months old, a little groggy from her nap and willing to be held by a sweaty, forty-one-year-old bearded man in bike shorts. And so we hung out a bit, bouncing around and watching Thomas and Becki move things from one place to another. "What are they doing?" she seemed to be asking me. "They don't know," I replied.

I was on a high when I left them to ride down Highway 100 back home. A good portion of the road, from the northern terminus of the Natchez Trace Parkway going east to Edwin Warner Park, has a soft shoulder ribbed with rumble strips. You can ride the thin space between the strips and the embankment, but it's not safe. There's scattered debris and garbage containers and opened mailboxes. It's a white-knuckled balancing act the whole way. Better to ride on the road, hugging the white line to the right.

I felt the white pickup truck creep up next to me, terribly close, and knew something bad was about to happen. He began to lean in, to direct the front of the truck toward the shoulder to force me off me the road. He pushed me onto the rumble strips, the bike shaking my body and chattering my jaw. I hopped to the right onto the space before the embankment, panicking and trying to steady myself. As he lurched forward, he pointed to the right to say, "Get over to the right," and sped off. I was furious. And scared. I never caught his license plate.

I stayed off Highway 100 for the next couple of weeks. I've had people yell out the window at me, buzz me, and, on one occasion, toss water out of a car. But never that. Never someone trying to kill me. It was the beginning of the cycling season, and I was jarred and shaken. I started mapping out alternative routes to the Natchez Trace Parkway. To Franklin. To Sophia.

A few weeks later, my writing group did an exercise that called for us to write briefly about something we had experienced that signaled the beginning of summer: no descriptions, no reflections, no color, no texture. Just the facts. So I jotted down a couple of sentences about the guy in the pickup truck who had tried to kill me. The second part of the exercise was to go back and fill in the details. To bring those facts to life and tell a story. I wrote about the temperature. The mocha. The ridge. The climbing. I wrote about Sophia. By the time the exercise ended, I hadn't even gotten to the guy.

Which means he hadn't gotten to me.

Faced with fleshing out the facts, I didn't immediately go to the guy who tried to run me off the road. I went to the baby who got me over the ridge. As I wrote, what I remembered of that day was not the fear that was still, to that very moment, gripping me. I remembered the warmth, and the innocence that inspired me.

12 HANDYMAN BLUES

There's a song by Billy Bragg on his album *Tooth & Nail* titled "Handyman Blues." In the song the narrator, presumably the singer, songwriter, and activist himself, rhapsodizes about his lack of proficiency when it comes to home repair. "Screwdriver business just gets me confused," he sings. "It takes me half an hour to change the fuse. And when I flicked the switch the lights all blew." And then the hook, "I'm not your handyman."

I relate to this song. But unlike Bragg's narrator, who's assured of himself as a writer, confident that his ideas "will turn to gold dust later," I haven't given up my handyman aspirations. I still believe I can fix things.

At this very moment, it's possible that my ex-wife is in the kitchen of the house in Brentwood, Tennessee where we both once lived—and that she now owns—standing under the track lighting that I installed. The same track lighting, she's likely to recall, that an electrician had to come over and make sure I did right after it started smoking a few days later. If she is, she's also near the gas range located under the track lighting. I cooked a lot of meals on that range, turning new knobs that I ordered from the parts store at Sears, and placing pots on burners that I cleaned by immersing them in a special solution that I also ordered from that same parts store at Sears. In the same conversation actually. I called to order the knobs, and we know how that goes.

If my ex-wife walks out of the kitchen area toward the half-bath and looks up to the second floor ceiling, she might see my handiwork around the HVAC vent. There were water stains around that vent and some peeling of the drywall when we moved in. I got up there shortly after, cut away the stained paper, and using drywall compound, seam tape and white paint, patched it. It looked terrible. But only if you looked closely and knew what you were looking for. Like most things in life.

One thing I do know is that the toilet bowl in the half-bath works. I installed it myself, in about an hour, with great personal fanfare. The victory came not long after my failure to install a new toilet bowl in the basement, and I really needed the win.

I'm not sure where my handyman aspirations come from. My dad was a decent amateur electrician, but I grew up in an apartment owned by my grandparents and never really learned how to fix anything. But still I tried. Toys, games, stereo equipment … and as I got older, computers and musical instruments. You name it, other than automobiles, I've tried to salvage it. I once kept a laptop going for about six years by calling HP and convincing the representative to send me the repair manual they normally only give to computer repair centers. "I'm completely comfortable with cracking open the back of the screen," I assured her.

I didn't live in a house that I was responsible for until I got married. But once I did, I took to it with gusto. I had a Home Depot do-it-yourself home maintenance manual, and a book dedicated entirely to plumbing, which I seemed to develop a special affinity for. It was of no help, though, when I decided to replace the shower knobs in the 1923 house in East Nashville where my ex-wife, Kathy, and I first lived. If it wasn't for my neighbor Bobby, all 80 years, six-feet-five inches and 90 pounds of him, we probably wouldn't have showered for a week.

I had no idea how incompetent at home repair Kathy thought I was until a meeting between the two of us and our attorneys during divorce negotiations. We had originally agreed to sell the house we shared, and because she was currently living in it, she made a list of all the repairs it needed before putting it on the market. Perusing the list, I suggested there were things that I could do, jobs I was certain I could handle or maybe that we could do together, that could save us a few bucks. She laughed, and then proceeded to openly detail for those in attendance my history of home improvement failure. I was being mocked, and it hurt. And while I could have defended myself, exercised my rights and insisted that I work on the house and save us that money, I conceded. It wasn't worth the fight. When she decided to keep the house and buy me out, perfect house that it now was after professional repairs, it hurt even more.

There are times when you need to own up to your own limitations. When you need to call in a professional plumber because a toilet installation in the basement of a house built on a concrete slab is not for amateurs. Or when the assistance of a neighbor who's almost as old as the house you're trying to fix is the closest you're going to get to an angel sent by God.

And then there are times when things are beyond repair. When the talents of even the most skilled plumber, electrician, or marriage counselor are useless. I needed that moment in the attorney's office. It was my reality check. My license to let go. To accept that there are some things you cannot fix.

Since my divorce, I've lived in rentals where once again I'm not responsible for repairs. But every now and then a faucet leaks and I get the urge to get my plumbing wrenches and test my skills. I've met someone, too, and I'm engaged to be married now. My fiancé, Keri, owns a little house of her own, and is capable of doing her own repairs. She even has a nice tool set to prove it. But on a recent visit I heard her toilet running and got a little excited. I opened up the tank to find a flapper in need of replacement and a tangled up chain. "I can fix this," I told her. In her kitchen, too, I discovered that the faucet lever was loose. "Do you have an Allen wrench set?" I asked.

We've been house shopping and preparing for a wedding, and sometimes I wonder if I'm ready. For the house. For the marriage. If I have the tools and possess the skills. And then I think about Billy Bragg's handyman. Maybe, like him, it's time to own up to my inabilities and accept that "I'm a writer not a decorator." But then I think about that toilet that I installed. The second one. The one I did correctly.

13 MEETING MERTON BESIDE THE MALL

As a Leonard Cohen[3] fan, I took it as a sign when Sister

---

[3] In a second floor apartment in a non-descript building on a street in the Heights section of Jersey City, on a wall likely hidden under coats of paint, is "The Only Poem" by Leonard Cohen. That is its title. "The Only Poem." I know it's there—unless, of course, the building has been knocked down or gutted—because I painted it. It was big, maybe three feet wide and five feet tall. I painted it with a small watercolor paintbrush and blue wall paint, starting at about 2 a.m. and finishing about 6 a.m.

It was the mid-nineties, I was in my mid-twenties, and that apartment was the first place I rented on my own. The rent was $450 a month. On the night I painted the poem, I was months into a serious bout of depression, deeper than I had ever experienced before. It was the kind of depression that we know well today. At work, and out socially with friends, I could be jovial and positive. No one would suspect I had depression. But alone, I struggled deeply. Unable to get myself out of bed, I saw no future for myself. I was overwhelmed by hopelessness and fear, and calmed only by the thought that no longer being alive might be the only way to make the pain go away. On the night I painted the poem, the depression had seized me like never before. I started to consider how I might acquire a gun. I wondered what pills might be best. I worried about who might find me and what might happen to my cats.

I don't know what moved in me, but in the middle of that night, I grabbed my copy of Leonard's song and poetry collection, Stranger Music. I flipped through looking for something, anything, to tide me over and get me through the night. And there it was. "The Only Poem."

> *This is the only poem*
> *I can read*
> *I am the only one*
> *can write it*
> *I didn't kill myself*
> *when things went wrong*
> *I didn't turn*
> *to drugs or teaching*
> *I tried to sleep*
> *but when I couldn't sleep*
> *I learned to write*
> *I learned to write*
> *what might be read*
> *on nights like this*
> *by one like me*

The poem spoke directly to me. Leonard had maybe been in the same exact place, and this was his letter to those who would follow him to that place. He learned to write, what might be read, on nights like this, by one like him. I needed that poem with me all the time. Every night. So I got up, found a small brush, and opened up one of the cans of paint I had used to paint the apartment doors and trim. It was painstakingly slow with the small brush. It took me all through the night and into the morning. And when it was finished, it was crooked and the lines weren't exactly written in the way Leonard has intended. But it was there, in the sunlight coming through the blinds. For hours, I was not hopeless. I did not think about ending my life. I thought about the poem, and I thought about writing.

Of course, you cannot write yourself out of serious clinical depression. That requires professional help and often medication. And with a reprieve, I soon took steps to find a doctor who diagnosed me and got me the help I needed. The depression would

Suzanne, from the Sisters of Mercy, returned my email.

I'd written earlier that week with an inquiry about the retreat she hosted at the Mercy Convent, a place for contemplation positioned within earshot of Opryland and Opry Mills mall in Nashville. I already had some idea, having grown up around nuns in Jersey City at my alma mater, St. Nicholas Grammar School.

"Mostly time and space for prayer," she'd replied.

I needed that time and space. Divorced only a few months after a long, contentious separation, I was starting my life over, and a weekend in silent contemplation seemed the perfect way to do it.

It was cold on that Friday morning in February—in the

---

return, in cycles in the years ahead, and fortunately, I always knew when I could no longer keep it at bay and needed to seek help.

But that poem certainly helped. It's not hyperbole to say it saved my life. I'm thankful to it to this day. And thankful to Leonard, who's since never been that far from me. I have a tattoo of the cover of his album, The Future, on my arm—a hummingbird lifting a heart free from its binds. And for a decade I carried in my wallet a copy of a passage from his book, Beautiful Losers, about what it means to be a saint. I only stopped carrying it because it disintegrated from being taken out and put back and read so much.

I have a photograph of the painting of the poem, and last night, after hearing of Leonard's death, I sent it my dear friend of 30 years, Kevin, who moved into that apartment after I moved out. He decided to keep the poem up for awhile, even if it was a little weird to his guests. It was certainly a conversation piece. It was he who mentioned that it might still be there, under many coats of paint. His exact words were that, "The Poem still lives under coats of paint." Lives. I liked that and suggested it was poetic all on its own.

There's an oft quoted lyric from Leonard's song, "Anthem," from the album, The Future: "There is a crack in everything / That's how the light gets in." He might be right. Maybe there's a poem behind everything, too.

I miss knowing Leonard walks among us. But I know he's still here.

mid-30s—when I set out on my bike from my West Nashville apartment to the convent. I had retrofitted my Bianchi Eros road bike with a rear rack and stuffed everything I needed into a trunk bag with attached panniers. It wasn't much. A pair of jeans, a couple of shirts, shoes, underwear, a notebook, rosary beads, and a book of Saint Pio of Pietrelcina's letters. Still, it weighed me down. Keeping the bike balanced at the red lights on Charlotte Pike heading east proved cumbersome, as did getting up off my saddle to climb hills. So I learned how to clip into my pedals while still seated. I took my time, watching out for the occasional patches of ice still on the ground from the recent and rare Nashville snowfall. I considered the mindfulness good preparation for the weekend.

I arrived before any of the other retreatants—how many were attending I didn't know—and was greeted by Sister Suzanne. I felt a little awkward at first in my tight-fitting bike kit, but I quickly became comfortable, especially when Sister Suzanne told me there was another gentleman who sometimes rides to the convent.

I told Sister Suzanne I found it wonderful that her name was Suzanne, like the title of the Leonard Cohen song, and that she was a Sister of Mercy, like the title of another Cohen song. I figured it was like women named Allison with the Elvis Costello song, or Gloria and Van Morrison. Or better yet, Mary and the entire Springsteen canon. Surely she knew the songs. But she didn't, and looked at me quizzically. I realized that Cohen was still a bit obscure, regardless of how many people covered his song, "Hallelujah," on *American Idol*. Or that maybe Sister Suzanne had dedicated her life to ambitions loftier than knowing the music of Canadian singer-songwriters from the late 60s. She'd been busy feeding the hungry and ministering to the poor.

My room was Spartan. Just a bed, a dresser, a chair, a night table and small bathroom. I set out my belongings, sat down, took a deep breath, and tried to figure out what to do with myself.

When I was younger, I independently studied Buddhism

and practiced mindfulness meditation. I was out of practice, but could still manage to wrangle and dismiss the thoughts flying through my mind, thirty to forty-five minutes at a time. I was prepared to mix Eastern and Western practices, including walking meditation, during the weekend. To devote this time, a stone's throw from the consumerism of Opry Mills, where silence is in short supply, felt almost subversive.

A half dozen other retreatants eventually arrived. I kept my head up in the hallway, ready to acknowledge a fellow traveler. We were all here for a reason, I assumed, in search of something. When a cyclist passes another cyclist coming toward them on the road, it's considered good form to wave or nod hello. Motorcyclists do the same thing, by flashing a two-finger, upside-down peace sign, to signal, "two wheels." I figured people on a retreat did something similar. I quickly learned that looking down and appearing in anguish was the thing.

In between meditation and prayer, and walking around the grounds of the convent counting my steps to the hum of Briley Parkway in the distance, I found the library. There was a young woman in there, and we ignored each other. I was learning.

What was I searching for? Mostly, I needed to know I was all right. That I was a good person. That I had tried my best. That I could get through what happened, and what was still happening, and come out on the other side.

I found Thomas Merton on the shelves. Merton was a Trappist monk at the Abbey of Gethsemani in Kentucky near Bardstown, about 150 miles north of Nashville. He was a Catholic writer and mystic, and while I knew of him, I had never read him. I chose *Life and Holiness*. With a blank journal to capture those passages that struck me, Merton became my confidante for the weekend.

"The way of perfection is not a way of escape," he wrote and I copied. "We can only become saints by facing ourselves, by assuming full responsibility for our lives just as they are, with all their handicaps and limitation, and submitting ourselves to the transforming action of the savior."

JOE PAGETTA

When the artist Salvador Dalí returned to Catholicism in the 1940s, late in his career, he referred to himself as a Catholic without faith. I understand a little of what Dalí was suggesting. I'm devout, but I'm not sure I believe in the "transforming action of the savior" that Merton is referring to, though I think I understand what the mystic means when he writes that "the Christian way of perfection is then, in every sense a way of life, of gratitude, of trust in God."

Maybe that's where that elusive transformation hides.

On the final day, after a morning mass, we were given an opportunity to meet with a Sister to talk about our experience at the retreat. At some point, joy had broken through my pain, and I told her so. There was much that had happened in the last few years that I could not control, and still more that I could not beat myself up about anymore. The retreat had brought that to light. I was going to be alright. She asked me if I had a personal relationship with Jesus. I asked her what she meant. She told me to spend time with his words and listen. I told her I'd been spending time with Merton.

I suited up in my bike kit, and stuffed all my belongings back into my trunk bag. It remained cold outside, and there was still ice on the ground, but the bike felt lighter and easier to manage. The 30 mile ride back to West Nashville, down Pennington Bend and McGavock Pike, along the Stones River and Shelby Bottom Greenways, across the Cumberland River, through Downtown Nashville and west up Charlotte Pike, was one of the most beautiful bike rides I have ever taken. I was gone only three days, but it felt like my city had changed.

In his song, "Sisters of Mercy," Cohen sings, "The Sisters of Mercy, they are not departed or gone. They were waiting for me when I felt that I could not go on. I hope you run into them, you who've been travelling so long."

14 REMEMBER ME?

My mother told me the other day that she hated me. It was not the strangest or most surprising thing she has done lately. My mother has taken to referring to me in the third person when we talk. Which makes all her false memories of conversations we had less untrue, I guess. Now it wasn't I who called her the night before and told her to wear her winter coat, as she imagined. Nor was it I who told her she didn't need to take her medicine anymore. "Joey" did.

Joey tells her a lot of ridiculous things. But of all the things I thought about this morning, while walking the 68 steps from the parking lot to the lobby of her senior community, her talking about me like I'm not here was not one of them. I take these steps every Sunday morning to pick her up. I think about things during the walk, but I also pray that it will be a good day. That I will have patience. That I will breathe. And that she and I will get along.

My mother is 71 and has dementia. Barring work or vacation, I try to see her every Sunday to take her to the Cathedral, out to lunch, and food shopping. I never know what I'm going to get with her each week, where her mind will be, or what she will be fixated on.

My mother's memory for what's coming up isn't bad. She writes everything down and knows when her doctor's appointments or hair appointments are. But she has very little recollection of having talked about anything. She overcompensates by continually filling in the space where that conversation should be. Everything she says is a segue from something else—either something we've talked about already, or something she thinks we have.

So everything begins with "and" and "so" and "yeah," as if we were just talking about it and hadn't finished. She will do this for as long as we're together, stringing together a conversation out of non sequiturs. During mass, I might be kneeling in my pew after receiving the Eucharist, reflecting, and she'll say, "Yeah, so the maintenance man said not to touch the thermostat." Or, "So Snoopy was under the bed when I left." Snoopy is her cat, which she laments naming Snoopy. Sometimes that comes up too.

My mother is adorable. Anyone who knows her will tell you that. She will tell you that. So I have a hard time reconciling the mother I know with the person who recently told me she hated me. She had a doctor's appointment coming up that she was fixating on, and didn't seem to understand that the doctor she was going to see was a psychiatrist and not an internist. I told her a thousand times that he didn't care about her cholesterol and blood thinner medicine, but she didn't seem to grasp it.

I know that ultimately she didn't need to grasp it, but I often find myself fixating, too, on trying to break through to her. Her psychiatrist had prescribed a medication to help her with her memory, and I told her he was going to ask her about it. Was she was taking it? She wouldn't give me a straight answer—claiming to not know what she takes—which is the dead giveaway that she's lying to me. Of course she knows what she takes. It's one of her fixations. So instead of answering, she told me she hated me.

It hurt. But I still took her for ice cream.

I could do a lot better being my mother's caretaker. There are things I should read, and newsletters I should subscribe to.

But it's hard enough understanding myself to try and understand her, or the illness that has so changed her. So I manage her money, pay her bills, take her to church and lunch and the grocery store. I can understand those things.

About five years ago she had a psychotic breakdown and wound up at Centennial Pavilion for a month. She told the intake nurse her health had been fine her whole life until she had me, which hurt in the same way her saying she hated me did. I went to the hospital every day I could and had lunch with her. She got better, was released, and for the past five years has stayed fairly stable, even as her brain function slowly declines. I found Snoopy for her on Craigslist, and taught her how to clean the litter box so she'd have something else to fixate on. But it gives her something to do, so I consider it a healthy fixation.

Sometimes she can be extremely lucid, and surprise me. Recently, I spent an afternoon at the film festival, where I used to handle media relations. While there, I was told a young female former associate was having a hard day and could use some comforting. I was trying to explain this to my mother the following day, and she smiled and said, "I think she was just using that as an excuse so you'd hold her." "You think?" I asked, and she laughed. 'Well, I didn't mind," I added. "I'm sure you didn't," she responded. She still has some Jersey in her.

We shared a small carrot cake at Panera that day for dessert. Taking the steps back to my car after dropping her off, I felt thankful that I had gotten through another Sunday. That Joey had gotten through another Sunday. I know my mother doesn't really hate either of us. She probably only hates the conversation she can't remember us having.

15 ART THAT WHISPERS FROM THE HALLWAY

In Donna Tartt's Pulitzer Prize-winning novel, *The Goldfinch*, I love the character of Hobie and the way he talks about art. There is a passage, very late in the novel, when Hobie explains to Theo why it is he thinks Carel Fabritius' painting, *The Goldfinch*, grabbed the young Theo the way it did.

> *"—if a painting really works down in your heart and changes the way you see, and think, and feel, you don't think, 'oh, I love this picture because it's universal.' 'I love this painting because it speaks to all mankind.' That's not the reason anyone loves a piece of art. It's a secret whisper from an alleyway. Psst, you. Hey kid. Yes you."*

Tartt, in a dismissal of the notion of the universal, has touched on the universal. We don't fall in love with books and paintings and albums and movies because they are somehow exemplary of the form. We fall in love because they speak to us. My sister once said to me—I was coming out of a long divorce and attempting to date again—that I didn't have to marry a woman just because she gave me a glass of water. Wise advice when you're parched. You can, though, give yourself entirely to a song the first time it speaks to you through your speakers. Or a painting when it spies you from across the gallery. Or a movie projected only toward you in a theatre. You don't have to feel guilty about the film you were with earlier in the week, either. Or the book that's still on your nightstand from the night before.

Tarrt's words, via Hobie, made me think about paintings that had that same effect on me, that said, "Psst, you. Yes, You." The painting I thought of first was George Bellow's *Portrait of Anne*. I first met it at the High Museum of Art in Atlanta the early 90s. I'm not sure what drew me to it initially other than it being adorable. Bellows was a master of light and texture, and the portrait, done later in his career and years after his success as a gritty urban realist, is an excellent example of his technique. Anne sits on wicker chair draped with a blue fabric, her skin soft and pale, her dress a bright white. Her golden hair is tied up in a light blue bow that repeats the color of the fabric. She looks like a porcelain doll. I loved the painting and her immediately. I wanted to be her father, asking her to help me with my craft, when she'd much rather be out playing with her friends or getting lost in storybooks. I learned later that Bellows used to pay Anne to sit for him, twenty-five cents an hour, which made the painting even more adorable to me. Her face took on a new dimension with this revelation, a cross between "I know I'm cute" and "Are you done yet? You're going to have to pay me another quarter any minute now."

I bought a print of the painting at the High Museum's store and took it back to New Jersey. I lived with my father then, and I hung it in our dining room. We didn't get along very well during this period, and I looked forward to the day I had the means to live on my own. When I finally did, I packed up all my belongings, and on the day I was to move, went to take the picture down. My father stopped me.

"Are you taking the picture?" he asked me.

"Why?" I wanted to know. "Do you want it?"

He did. He liked it, he said. In all the time we shared

together in the apartment while the print hung in the dining room, we never discussed it. He never asked me about it or where I got it. He didn't know that Bellows paid his daughter twenty-five cents to sit for him. And yet, like me, he was drawn to it. It spoke to him.

And so I left it for him. Maybe it reminded him of his daughter, my sister, when she was younger. Maybe all those nights when he was sitting alone in the living room, smoking cigarettes and watching television, he was glancing over into the dining room and drawing some comfort from Anne's cautious smile. I won't ever know why he liked it, because even though our relationship improved before he died in 2007, we never talked about it. We didn't really need to.

Sometimes, as Tartt suggests, it's "a secret whisper," from an alleyway, around a gallery corner, or from the dining room. I understood that.

16 WHO WANTS TO READ ABOUT BROKEN ARMS?

A few years ago, on the 50th Anniversary of Harper Lee's *To Kill a Mockingbird*, I decided to reread the novel for the first time since high school. Being a classic novel that I was certain even my mother had read, I suggested we read it together in some kind of mother/son book club. Within a week, my mother gave it up. "Too depressing," she said. " Who wants to read about broken arms?"

She clearly hadn't gotten very far.

A curious result of my mother's early onset dementia is an aversion to anything even remotely depressing. She doesn't remember having estate arguments with her family after her stepmother died or getting divorced from my father. She doesn't remember struggling and working two and three jobs at a time to make ends meet and live on her own. And she doesn't remember getting sick herself and going on disability after years of helping the aged and bedridden as a visiting homemaker. I had given her a Billy Crystal book years before the birth of the mother/son book club, and she seemed to like that. So perhaps I should have chosen something lighter for our inaugural read.

My thinking behind the book club was two-fold. One, reread the book, and two, bond with my mother over something I've given her the bulk of the credit for in my life: my love of books. I thought sharing in something she instilled in me would give us a new way to navigate what was surely going to be rocky terrain as her dementia progressed.

From my earliest days being dropped off at the Zabriskie Street branch of the Jersey City public library, I have found a comfort in books. I like to be around them. To always be reading them. I carry one with me just in case I have a moment to read it, even on busy days when I know I won't have the opportunity. And for this I credit my mother.

She was the one who dropped me off at the library. In between screenings of Disney's *The Jungle Book* and arts and crafts classes where we made kazoos out of toilet paper rolls, I read books. I took stacks of them home with me, each stamped with the date they needed to be returned, and each with a corresponding card that now had a record of the fact that I, Joe Pagetta, had turned its pages. When the Scholastic Books Catalog came out, my mother encouraged me to choose copies of *The Swiss Family Robinson* and *Treasure Island* to add to my own collection. One Christmas, she didn't hesitate when I eschewed GI Joes and Masters of the Universe characters and told her all I wanted was to go up to Garden State News on Central Avenue and pick up copies of *The Adventures of Huckleberry Finn* and *Robinson Crusoe* and whatever else my personal library was lacking.

That I can't share with my mother my passion for something she is partly responsible for is sometimes difficult, a vivid reminder of her disease. When my wife Keri and I moved into our new house, we invited my mother to come over and see what we had done with the place. The new office/library was crammed with books, overflowing in front of and on top of the insufficient number of bookcases we had decided to move.

"Joey and his books," my mother said. "He's always had a lot of books. Why do you need all these books?"

"It's my personal library," I assured her. "And you're the one that's responsible for it."

I reminded her about Zabriskie Street, and Garden State News. And while she remembered the library, she didn't immediately make the connection as to what they had to do with all the books in my house. I think she even said something like, "yeah, you're supposed to bring them back," but that could have easily been my wife ribbing me as well.

And then I had an idea. I pulled down my old paperback copies of *Huckleberry Finn* and *Tom Sawyer* from the shelf, and showed her the inside of the covers. There, in black rubber stamp ink, sans serif font, was my full name and the street address where I grew up, where we once lived as a family.

I think that's when it hit her. I had some of these books for over 30 years. I still had those books she bought me at Garden State News. When I was building my personal library, and stacking them in the cabinet in the furnace room in the basement of the house where I was raised, I figured a proper library needed a library stamp. So I had one made. I didn't know about bookplates and the various other professional ways to mark books, so I got a basic return address rubber stamp, and stamped the inside covers of all my books.

There have been times when I've moved in the last two decades and wondered why I lugged around all these books. Why, even after dropping off boxes of books at the library and Goodwill, there were still some books I couldn't part with. What value is there in some generic Penguin paperback version of John Steinbeck's *Of Mice and Men* or James Joyce's *Dubliners*? And why, when browsing a used bookstore, did I get excited about a pristine paperback copy of H.G. Wells' *The Invisible Man*, an exact copy of the one I had as a kid. I always thought it was because at some point my son or daughter, or grandson or granddaughter, might come home from school and tell me they were reading Rousseau or Plato or Nietzsche, and I could say, "Oh, I have that right here." Or maybe they were embarking on Joyce or Hemingway or Fitzgerald and I could tag along. I still think those are valid justifications, even in a digital world. But I think there are other reasons now, too. Reasons that didn't exist even a decade ago.

My mother and I may never read a book together again, and thinking back, I'm not certain we ever really did. But she's with me in every volume I pull off the shelf in my personal library—whether in the rubber stamp on the inside cover, in the fond memory of her letting me pick whatever I wanted in the bookstore, or in her voice every time I bring her over my house for lunch and she wonders why I have all these books.

17 HONEY AND A HAM SANDWICH

If I'm ever in the unfortunate situation of having to choose my last meal, I will choose a ham sandwich on lightly-toasted Pepperidge Farm bread and a cup of tea with milk and sugar. This is what I ate for lunch with my grandmother most afternoons when I was in grammar school. I went to St. Nicholas in the Heights section of Jersey City, which was only a few blocks away from the house where we lived—my mom, dad, brother, and sister on the top floor; my grandmother and grandfather on the first floor. My grandfather died when I was eight, right around the age that I started walking to and from school myself. My grandmother, whom I called Nanny, would usually have the sandwich and tea ready for me when I got home. We'd chat about whatever was on either of our minds, and then she'd send me back to school with a quarter. There was a grocery store on the corner in between my house and school, and I'd use the quarter to pick up a bag of Wise potato chips on the way back.

Nanny wasn't my real grandmother, but she was the only grandmother I knew. My father's parents died before I was born. My mother's mother died when she was 14 due to complications from gallbladder surgery. My mother's father, with two teenage daughters, one of them with an intellectual disability, and two younger sons, knew he needed help and that his children needed a mother. He met and married Mary, whom he and my mother and her siblings called Mae, about three years later. She was an extraordinary woman. Already a professional, she worked for the International Telephone & Telegraph (ITT) company in Manhattan. She became a mentor to my mother and introduced her to New York and the arts and helped her get her first job, as a personal secretary at JP Morgan. She may have never given birth to children, but certainly loved my mother and her siblings as her own.

It was the same with her grandkids. She took full advantage of our proximity to New York and would pack us and our friends in her late 70s blue Nova to take us to Liberty State Park in downtown Jersey City, and onto the ferries to Ellis Island and The Statue of Liberty. It didn't occur to me then—I figured we needed something to do in the summer and she was happy to be our chaperone—she probably had a strong sense of shared history and that was her way of introducing it to us. Like us, she was of Italian descent. Her ancestors were greeted by the same The Statue of Liberty and came through the same Ellis Island as ours did. We may not have been blood, but we came from the same blood.

She was funny, too, especially on these field trips, even though we drove her crazy. One time, she rear-ended another driver on the way back to the house. The guy got out of the car, came up to her driver's side window, and started screaming at her in Spanish. None of us knew what he was saying, but she calmly pulled a five dollar bill out of her purse and told him, in English, to go buy himself a soda. He was flummoxed and got silent. He took the money and walked back to his car.

Nanny died when I was 19, due to complications from a brain tumor. My mother, with whatever help my sister and I could provide, took care of her for as long as she could while she lay in a hospital bed in her living room. Our lunchtime ritual had stopped long ago, but her death was a blow to my and my family's life that in many ways we never recovered from. My mother's family fell apart and my parents divorced. Me and my siblings went our separate ways. Looking back, it's clear that my mother's mood disorder, diagnosed years later along with early onset dementia, was already present.

I've long known that a ham sandwich on lightly-toasted Pepperidge farm bread and a cup of tea with milk and sugar would be my preferred last meal, but it's only now that I realize why. Sure, it's a comfort food, taking me back to those charming afternoons with Nanny. But it's also the taste of "before." Before estrangement. Before dementia. Before experience.

My wife and I have one-year-old twin girls that were conceived with the aid of an egg donor. Late last year, my mother-in-law moved in with us. It's a mutually beneficial arrangement. She has her own room and bathroom on one side of the house, and we have built-in help in the mornings and evenings before and after work. We both save money. There are less tangible benefits, too, like the joy my mother-in-law experiences every time she walks out of her room in the morning or into the house after she gets off work and sees those two smiling faces staring back at her.

The biggest winners are my daughters, who get to spend time with Honey, as she prefers to be called, in the way I got to spend time with Nanny. Fridays belong only to them, and when they get together, there is always plenty of babbling going back and forth. Like Nanny, Honey may not be blood, but you'd never know it.

Times have changed and eating ham on lightly-toasted Pepperidge Farm white bread and following it with a bag of chips every day is no longer an acceptable lunch. Even if Honey, who's a bit old school, disagrees. We're somewhat lucky that the girls can't truly eat solid food yet. But there's a Catholic grammar school around the corner from where we live that I hope we can afford and the girls can attend in a few years. Maybe some things haven't entirely changed.

We all have a "before" and an "after" in our lives. William Blake pointed that out in the 18th Century. I wish my daughters wouldn't have to have an "after," but at least I know they're having the sweetest "before" I can imagine.

APPENDIX

In Italy

We met on Franklin Street in the Heights section of Jersey City. It was the night before I moved to Nashville, and my father had asked me to meet him at the club where he frequently played cards with his friends from the old country. We each had an espresso, and then we took a walk. Not far from the club, he handed me a thousand dollars and said he wished he could give me more. He told me to be careful. He hugged me. As I walked back to my car, I tried to control my breathing and hold back the tears. Something was ending, and something was beginning, but there was much I was leaving unfinished.

My father wasn't endorsing this move. In the months leading up to it, he told me several times how stupid I was. He couldn't understand it. It wasn't until I reminded him that he was around my age, twenty-six, when he left Italy to find a better life in America. He had traveled across an ocean to another continent; I was merely moving south, about 900 miles. I too was trying to find a better life, and maybe some success as a singer-songwriter in the process.

He came around, but his new understanding couldn't make

up for the past twenty-six years. My father had problems with gambling, but he worked long hours, and to him that was enough: as long as there was a roof over our heads, clothes on our bodies, and food on the table, he was doing his job, never mind that he was also verbally abusive and physically violent.

I was ten years old the first time I heard my mother mention divorce. She waited another nine years before finally getting one. My brother dealt with my father by fighting back. My sister alternated between taunting him and taking the blows. I figured the best way to handle my father, outside of those times when I didn't have a choice, was to avoid him. I retreated to my books and my records and created an alternate world in my head.

My first year in Nashville was difficult. When you're Italian American and you've lived your entire life in northeast New Jersey, Nashville in those days could be a lonely place. Gigs were hard to come by, and money was tight. I had moved to Nashville with my girlfriend, and our relationship was falling apart. I was out of my element. Who I was, and where I was from, quickly went from being something I took for granted to something I was in danger of losing.

A year later, in late 1999, my Uncle Pinuccio (Giuseppe) passed away in Italy. My father hadn't been home in fifteen years, and I convinced him he needed to go back. I even told him that I would join him. He surprised me by suggesting a longer trip: instead of going directly to Pisticci in the south of Italy, we would start our trip in the northern city of Milan and ride the train all the way down. He thought it would make the visit more worthwhile for me if we saw Venice, Florence, and Rome and visited all the tourist stops along the way. It was a risky proposition. The entire trip would take almost three weeks.

The ups and downs and triumphs and tribulations of that trip are a whole other story, one that I fortunately detailed each day in a journal. While we certainly had our fights—he was miserable during most of the time we spent north of Rome— we were also forced, through close quarters in hotel rooms and on trains, to get to know each other. Each meal was a chance for me to explain who I was and what I cared about and what I hoped to accomplish. Each walk in a city square was a chance for my father to tell me about not only what frustrated him but also what made him proud—things he had never said to me before.

Our arrival in Pisticci was triumphant. I visited with my uncles and cousins and got to see my father in a completely different way, on the very streets where he had grown up. An airline strike on the day we were to depart gave us one more perfect evening to walk and talk in the Adriatic Sea town of Bari.

Everything changed after that trip. Over the next seven years, we talked often on the phone, and he even came to visit me one Thanksgiving. I never achieved great songwriting success, but I continued to perform, traveling back to New York and New Jersey for several gigs each year. In 2004, he came to see me play—for the first time ever—at a show in Asbury Park. His only complaint was that I didn't play longer.

More than eighty percent of lung cancers are already in Stage IV when they're discovered. My father's, diagnosed in September 2007, was no exception. I flew up to New Jersey as soon as I heard, and together my sister and I jumped into action, making appointments, reading up on cancer, and mentally preparing ourselves, and our father, for the fight ahead. But the fight didn't last long. By early November, he was moved into intensive care, where he slipped into a coma. Forty-eight hours later, and less than two months after his diagnosis, with me holding one hand and my sister holding the other, he passed away.

I had been preparing for my father's death for almost ten years. There was nothing I needed to say to him that he didn't know. There was nothing he needed to say to me. Years earlier, we had taken a chance to love one another, to build a new relationship because we both knew we couldn't change the past. We succeeded.

CREDITS

Many of these essays found previous homes in publications and performances. I'm grateful to those hosts that invited me to read, and editors who believed in me and made my work the best it could be.

"Art That Whispers from the Hallway" was originally published at *Nashville Arts* (http://nashvillearts.com).

"Centerfold" was originally read at Howlin' After Dark at Howlin' Books in Nashville.

"Handyman Blues" was originally read at Howlin' After Dark.

"Honey and a Ham Sandwich" was originally published at Chapter 16 (http://www/chapter16.org).

"In Italy" was originally published at *Chapter 16*.

"On Being a Queen Fan: The Days before the Day that Changed the World" was workshopped at a Nashville State Tech Community College creative writing class and originally published in abridged form in *Bohemian Rhapsodies: True And Authorized Tales By Queen Fans & Celebrities* by Robyn Dunford, Rock N Roll Books.

"Reality Shows" was originally read at Howlin' After Dark.

"Remember Me?" was originally published in the *Nashville*

Scene (http://www.nashvillescene.com).

"Sleeping on Couches" was workshopped at a Watkins College of Art Community Education creative writing class and originally published at *Chapter 16*.

"Spilt Milk" was originally read of Howlin' After Dark.

"Two Wheels and the Truth" was originally published at *Chapter 16*.

"Wet Behind the Ears" was originally read at Howlin' After Dark.

"Where Were You?" was originally published in the *Nashville Scene*.

"Who Wants to Read About Broken Arms?" was originally read at Howlin' After Dark.

JOE PAGETTA

ACKNOWLEDGEMENTS

I was in Italy, coincidentally, when my essay, "In Italy," included here in the appendix, was published in the Humanities Tennessee online literary magazine, *Chapter 16*. It was June, 2011. The story had been bouncing around my inbox since at least 2008, when it was written for a compilation of personal essays called *Love Wins* that was never published. It's about a trip — referenced here in the essay, "Mussolini and Me" — that I took to Italy with my father in 2000. I thought what my father and I accomplished on that trip, and in our lives, was quite extraordinary. I certainly felt that love did indeed win.

In 2011, I was alone, on a cycling trip through the Veneto region in Northern Italy, close to the Alps. It was the only way I could figure to deal with the dissolution of my first marriage, and maybe love not winning. Newly separated, and living in a strange rental house, I decided to go to Italy and ride my bike. I didn't know anyone there. I wasn't sure of my cycling skill level. But it made sense to me.

The experience was life-altering and leg-burning. But as much as I wanted that trip to clear my heart and mind, and provide some epiphany at the top of some grueling mountain climb (the climb turned out to be Monte Grappa), it was the publishing of that essay, after years of it looking for a home, that provided the greatest directive: write.

I wrote professionally all the time, and had been for years. I was a publicist, and wrote press releases on deadline. I wrote blog posts for work. Speeches. The occasional op-ed piece for the local paper. I knew I could write effectively, and took pride in my abilities and craftsman-like approach.

I got my first professional job as a writer when I was 17, as a paid intern in the sports department of my local newspaper. By 19, I was on the staff, moving on to news and lifestyle reporting. I was in college at the same time, writing for and editing my school papers. After taking a break from newspaper work, I dabbled in corporate communications and marketing before establishing myself in public relations.

By the time I took that the cycling trip, I figure I had been telling other people's stories for almost two decades. Perhaps it was time I tried to tell my own.

So I started writing more stories and submitting them for publication. I took creative nonfiction writing classes in the evenings at local colleges. I joined a writing group that met twice a month, and got invited to read my work at writers nights.

That's where the majority of the pieces in this collection come from. Some were workshopped over several weeks in class, some came from writing prompts on a single night.

Writing helped me put things in perspective, and explore a past and a present that were never far from each other. Faulkner knew it all along, of course. Writing helped me recognize that the old neighborhood that I escaped in my mid-20s was still with me. That was a very good thing. That growing up in a house with parents who were always fighting could actually be helpful as an adult, especially when you realize that misery is a cycle. I was reminded that books and music matter. They provided friendship and guidance all these years, and instilled in me sensibilities that weren't readily available. They opened up the world. They represented possibility.

In writing these stories, I remembered, too, that we have to laugh. Some of what seemed so horrible back then, some of that misery that seemed so oppressive, is actually pretty funny. I probably laughed more in the last five years than I laughed in my first 40.

According to writer Leo Buscaglia, "Ancient Egyptians believed that upon death they would be asked two questions and their answers would determine whether they could continue their journey in the afterlife. The first question was, 'Did you bring joy?' The second was, 'Did you find joy?'"

I like to think with this collection, I've said "yes" to both of these questions.

I'm thankful for the many people in these last five years that encouraged me to write, published a piece or asked me to read. They include Margaret Renkl at *Chapter 16* for editing and publishing that first piece and others after; the late Jim Ridley at the *Nashville Scene*; Jack Silverman at the *Nashville Scene*; Paul Polycarpou at *Nashville Arts Magazine*; Gloria Ballard at Watkins College of Art; Randy Rudder at Nashville State; the late Merrill Farnsworth, leader of the Writing Circle, and all my fellow Circle writers, including Carl, Dee, Mark, Jamie, John and Tara. Thanks to my editor, Maria Browning, who gave a first look at this collection and offered thoughtful guidance, encouragement and advice moving forward, and then gave it an deeper look when I decided I was ready to publish it. Thanks to early readers who took time out of their busy lives to offer perspective and opinions, including Mary Laura Philpott, Kim Greene and David Fioccola. Thank you to musician, producer, and graphic artist, Sam Smith (samsmyth.net), for his creativity and enthusiasm in designing the book jacket. I'm honored he agreed to work with me. Special thanks to my sister, Mary, for always reading my work and helping me get my facts straight. She also loves me like only a sister can. To my mom, for teaching me compassion, and introducing me to books. Special thanks to my wife, Keri, for listening to many of these pieces in their first drafts, and providing guidance when it was time to read them. It's Keri, as well, who gets credit for the above Buscaglia quote. She introduced it to me, and reminds me every day of the value in living it.

JOE PAGETTA

GUINEA BASTARD

JOE PAGETTA

GUINEA BASTARD

The young writer at home in Jersey City, New Jersey, c. 1982.

JOE PAGETTA

ABOUT THE AUTHOR

Born and raised in Jersey City, New Jersey, Joe Pagetta is a writer and nonprofit communications professional whose personal essays and arts writings have appeared in *America: The Jesuit Review*, *Nashville Arts*, *Nashville Scene*, *Chapter 16*, *PBS.org* and—if you count the time it published an excerpt of his letter to novelist Colum McCann about his fashion sense—*Esquire*. A cycling enthusiast, amateur chef and book collector, he is a founding member of The Men of La Mangia and The Queen Breakfast Club, and for many years, was the namesake of a sandwich at Savarino's Cucina in Nashville. He lives in Nashville, Tennessee with his wife, twin daughters, and dog and cat. More at joepagetta.com.

98446299R00062

Made in the USA
Columbia, SC
25 June 2018